BRAZIL

GOOD STORIES REVEAL as much, or more, about a locale as any map or guidebook. Whereabouts Press is dedicated to publishing books that will enlighten a traveler to the soul of a place. By bringing a country's stories to the English-speaking reader, we hope to convey its culture through literature. Books from Whereabouts Press are essential companions for the curious traveler, and for the person who appreciates how fine writing enhances one's experiences in the world.

"Coming newly into Spanish, I lacked two essentials—a childhood in the language, which I could never acquire, and a sense of its literature, which I could."

—Alastair Reid, *Whereabouts: Notes on Being a Foreigner*

OTHER TRAVELER'S LITERARY COMPANIONS

Amsterdam	*Ireland*
Argentina	*Israel*
Australia	*Italy*
Chile	*Japan*
China	*Mexico*
Costa Rica	*Prague*
Cuba	*South Africa*
France	*Spain*
Greece	*Vienna*
India	*Vietnam*

BRAZIL

A TRAVELER'S LITERARY COMPANION

EDITED BY

ALEXIS LEVITIN

WHEREABOUTS PRESS
BERKELEY, CALIFORNIA

Copyright © 2010 by Whereabouts Press

Preface © 2010 by Alexis Levitin
(complete copyright information on page 241)

Map of Brazil by BookMatters

ALL RIGHTS RESERVED

Published by
Whereabouts Press
Berkeley, California
www.whereaboutspress.com

Distributed to the trade by PGW / Perseus Distribution

No part of this book may be reproduced in any form or by any electronic
or mechanical means, including information storage and retrieval sys-
tems, without permission in writing from the publisher, except by a re-
viewer, who may quote brief passages in a review.

MANUFACTURED IN THE UNITED STATES OF AMERICA

Library of Congress Cataloging-in-Publication Data

Brazil : a traveler's literary companion / edited by Alexis Levitin.
p. cm.
ISBN 978-1-883513-21-4 (alk. paper)
1. Short stories, Brazilian—Translations into English.
2. Brazilian fiction—20th century—Translations into English.
3. Brazil—In literature.
I. Levitin, Alexis.
PQ9677.E5B73   2009
869.3'010835881—dc22   2009038792

5 4 3 2 1

Contents

THE SOUTH

Foreword

Gregory Rabassa

The isle of Serendip was said to be Ceylon (or Taprobana or Sri Lanka) but it also could have been Brazil, because it too was discovered by the Portuguese and was taken to be an island at the time. Although it has never been admitted officially—and most likely never will—serendipity and happenstance seem to be a mainstay of Brazil's history from its very start, when Cabral supposedly stumbled upon it on his way to India. Even its name was not what they called it in earliest times. It came to be called *Brazil* in Portugal because of the colony's wealth of the fine hardwood tree called brazilwood.

The language itself wandered off from the standard tongue in a manner of some kind of linguistic Darwinism, although far from any kind of theoretical rigidity. Brazilian Portuguese says what is best to be said at the moment or maybe just what it wants to say. In spite of this and many other freedoms, Brazil has managed to survive as a country, perhaps because of this same brand of individualism that quietly says "Why not?" The spirit behind all this is what the Brazilians call *jeito*, the impossible-to-translate word which seems to mean whatever they want it to mean. As we go from north to south, or from one region or city to another, the very separation of customs and manners is what holds them together as a nation: the paradox of jeito.

When reading things Brazilian it is wise not to plug them into universal literary currents, even when the authors themselves say this is where their muse lies. It is better to look at them side by side with other Brazilian things, looking past the words themselves to see what makes them siblings. The same can be done with buildings, paintings, and music as we seek out a common essence. And most often it will be the originality that is born of the moment. This is what you will find in these writings as you read them, while contemplating or unconsciously synthesizing what is around you or has been around you or will be around you in this variegated and free-spirited scene that is called Brazil.

Preface

I want to keep this preface short, allowing the stories to tell themselves, unmediated.

Brazil is the fifth largest country in the world, occupying nearly half of South America. It pulsates with life. It percolates death. Everywhere there seems to be more of everything, all of it intertwined, like a mangrove swamp, like a rainforest draped in lianas.

How to capture it all? How to be representative?

It can't be done. And so this mini-preface is a confession. There is something arbitrary about any anthology. This one owes a great deal to chance. In his foreword, Gregory Rabassa is right to focus on the word *serendipity*, "the faculty of making happy and unexpected discoveries by accident." It is my hope that this book will prove itself a kind of paean of praise to serendipity.

The stories in this collection are presented by region, with the initial focus on Brazil's two major cities, Rio de Janeiro and São Paulo. Their friendly rivalry in the Brazilian imagination is depicted with a light ironic touch in the first story of the book, Luis F. Verissimo's "The Real José." After Rio and São Paulo, the reader, heading in any direction, will encounter Brazil's ebullience, humor, sen-

suality, passion, abundance, tenderness, and the menace
of violence.

Beyond the organizing principle of geography, this is
an unprincipled anthology. I hope its richness of disor-
der and diversity mirrors that of the country itself. As
for the authors represented and the stories selected, the
anthologist must fall back upon the truth: serendipity.
Some authors are world famous icons (Machado de Assis,
Jorge Amado), some are newcomers, still little known
even in their own country. Many of the stories are urban,
others rural, some almost epically primordial. Some resonate with irony, irreverence, satire. Others speak in the
rhythms of myth and tragedy. Some of these stories were
drawn from my own earlier translation projects, others
from previous anthologies. And, of course, numerous
friends and colleagues, to whom I am deeply grateful,
have contributed to this collection.

But whatever its sources, in the end this anthology lays
no claim to being comprehensive or definitive. Rather it
seeks to give the reader a glimpse here and there of a rich
and bewildering land and its people. Editorial decisions
have relied upon one very simple principle: the pleasure
principle—mine and, if all goes well, your own. I hope
that the literary traveler in Brazil will savor this book as a
rich and textured seasoning to the land itself.

Alexis Levitin
September 2009
PLATTSBURGH, NEW YORK

The Real José

Luis Fernando Verissimo

JOSÉ DIED—with some poetic justice—on the air shuttle between São Paulo and Rio. His heart gave out. He died wearing a gray suit and a dark tie and clutching the same black briefcase with which he had disembarked at Rio's Santos Dumont airport every Monday for years. Except that this time, the black briefcase had been placed on his chest, as he lay on the stretcher, like a provisional headstone.

LUIS FERNANDO VERISSIMO was born in 1936 in Porto Alegre, Rio Grande do Sul, where he still lives. He has written four novels and many collections of short stories. His regular columns—or *crónicas*—have become a regular and much-loved feature in many of Brazil's major national newspapers. He is also a celebrated cartoonist and plays saxophone in a local jazz band. Verissimo has a wonderfully bittersweet sense of humor and, as this story illustrates, is a wry commentator on contemporary Brazilian mores. Two of his novels *The Club of Angels* and *Borges and the Eternal Orangutans* have been translated into English.

"Poor old Paulista," said his colleagues at the wake, regretting the loss of such a serious, efficient, hard-working companion. His nickname in Rio was Paulista.

His wife and eighteen-year-old son maintained a look of sober resignation during the wake. That had always been José's style. No emotional outbursts and no displays of sentiment. Sobriety. It was his son's idea that they should bury him wearing his waistcoat.

"The fact is," whispered one of José's associates at work, "he never really adapted to the *carioca* way of life."

"Yes, he was always a *paulista* in exile," commented someone else.

"In exile?" asked another. "But he lived in both places, in Rio and São Paulo."

It was then that two women, one older, one younger, burst in on the wake, sobbing, both of them wearing the same style jeans and both carrying the large leather bags with which they had traveled from São Paulo.

"Carioca!" cried the older woman, rushing towards the coffin. "Is it really you, Carioca?"

"Papa!" cried the younger woman, hurling herself on the solemn corpse.

General consternation.

Dr. Lupércio, the family's lawyer, finally managed to hustle José's two wives into an area some way away from the room in which the wake was being held. The most difficult part was removing wife number two—in order of arrival at the wake—from on top of the coffin. The truth soon became plain. José had another family in São Paulo. His daughter was fifteen. The Rio wife came straight to the point:

"I'm his legal wife."

"My dear . . . " began the other woman.

"Don't you 'my dear' me. We don't even know each other."

"Please, keep calm," begged Dr Lupércio.

"Now I know why Carioca never wanted to bring me to Rio," said the other wife.

"His name is José, or at least it was, until this happened," said the first wife, leaving it unclear as to whether by "this" she was referring to his death or to the revelation that he had another family.

"In São Paulo, the gang all call him Carioca."

"The 'gang'?" said the first wife, bemused. In Rio they certainly didn't belong to a "gang." They rarely went out. Apart from the occasional supper with a few close friends. And the odd concert. But generally they were in bed by ten.

At the wake, José's son avoided meeting his half-sister's gaze. Physically, they were very alike. They had their father's features. The girl, her eyes still brimming with tears, remarked that this was the first time she had seen her father wearing a tie. The son was about to say that he couldn't remember ever seeing his father *without* a tie, but thought it best to say nothing. It was all so very awkward.

"Poor Papa," said the girl, sobbing. "He was always so full of life."

The son felt more and more confused.

José's nickname in São Paulo was Carioca. He got off the plane at São Paulo's Congonhas airport each Thursday, wearing a T-shirt. With perhaps a sweater draped over his shoulders. Once, he'd even arrived wearing bermudas and thongs. He liked to fill the apartment with friends or to go out with the gang to a restaurant or a nightclub. And if anyone threatened to leave early, saying they had to work the next day, he would declare that *paulistas* simply didn't know how to live, that *paulistas* thought only of money, that only *cariocas* knew how to enjoy life to the full. His cheerful informality was a great success among *paulistas*, even though, at business meetings, the way he wore his shirt unbuttoned to the navel always caused a certain unease. Every Monday, he would fly back to Rio, saying that he needed to get in a bit of beach-time and chill out.

"Didn't you find it odd that he always came back from Rio looking so pale?" asked the first wife.

"He always said that he lost any tan he'd picked up at the beach the moment he set foot in São Paulo airport," said the other wife.

They both smiled.

Later, at home, Dr. Lupércio reflected on the matter.

"A hero of two worlds," he declared.

His wife, as usual, wasn't listening. Dr. Lupércio went on:

"In Rio, he was the typical *paulista*, a caricature really! Yes, that's it!"

Dr. Lupércio always got very excited when he plucked an idea out of the air with his long fingers. That was it! In Rio, he was a caricature of a *paulista*. The *carioca*'s image of what a *paulista* should be. And in São Paulo, he was the opposite.

"More than that, when he played the role of the proverbial *paulista* in Rio, he was having a bit of fun, but when he played the *carioca* in São Paulo, it was a sales tactic."

In his enthusiasm, Dr. Lupércio squeezed his wife's arm hard. "Ow!" she squealed.

"Don't you see? He was being a typically wily, idle *carioca* when he played the *paulista*, and a typically utilitarian *paulista* when he played the *carioca*. A gigolo of national stereotypes! A Brazilian synthesis! But which of the two was the real José?"

The two widows went to bed alone. The Rio widow without her José—that rock of solid values and responsibilities in the midst of *carioca* fecklessness; the São Paulo widow without her Carioca—that breath of sea air blowing through the *paulista* grayness.

The two women sighed.

Translated by Margaret Jull Costa

The Wallet

Machado de Assis

...SUDDENLY, HONÓRIO looked down and saw a wallet on the ground. To bend over, pick it up, and put it in his pocket was a matter of seconds. No one had seen him, save for a stranger in a shop doorway, who said, laughing:

"Good thing you found it when you did, or it'd be lost for ever."

"True enough," agreed Honório, embarrassed.

JOAQUIM MARIA MACHADO DE ASSIS (1839–1908) lived his whole life in Rio de Janeiro. He was a typesetter, a proofreader, a journalist, and became the first president of the Brazilian Academy of Letters in 1896. He left behind a vast body of work including poetry, short stories, and novels, which were immensely popular in Brazil. Although he did not achieve worldwide acclaim in his lifetime, he is now heralded as one of the greatest writers of the 19th century. His works are famous for their irony, psychological insight, and pessimistic outlook on human nature. He is best known for the eccentric first-person narrative in *The Posthumous Memoirs of Bras Cubas* (1881) and the novels *Philosopher or Dog?* (1891) and *Dom Casmurro* (1899), widely considered his masterpiece.

To understand the opportunity afforded by the wallet, one should know that Honório had to pay a debt the next day, four hundred and something *mil-reis*, and the wallet was bulging. It may not seem so great a debt for a man of such standing, who practiced law, but all sums are great or small according to circumstance, and his could not have been worse. Excessive family expenses, first to help relatives, then to please his wife, who was weary of solitude; a ball here, a dinner there, hats, fans, so many other things that there was no remedy but to borrow from the future. He got into debt. It began with tabs in shops and grocery stores; then loans, two hundred from one person, three hundred from another, five hundred from another, and it all kept growing, and there were parties to be thrown, and dinners to be eaten, a constant spiral, a vortex.

"You're doing well now, aren't you?" Gustavo C., lawyer and family friend, had said recently.

"I am now," Honório lied.

Truth be told, he was doing badly. Only a handful of cases, poorly paid, and not settled on time. As luck would have it, he'd recently lost a case in which he'd invested great hopes. Not only had he earned little from it, but it also seemed to have cost him something of his legal reputation; the newspapers, at least, hadn't been kind.

His wife Amélia knew nothing; he kept her in the dark concerning his business, good or bad. He told no one anything. He made a show of being cheerful, as if he were swimming in a sea of prosperity. When Gustavo, who came to visit every evening, told a joke or two, he'd come back with three or four; and then he'd listen to the German pieces that Amélia played so well on the piano, and which Gustavo drank in with indescribable pleasure, or they'd play cards, or simply talk politics.

One day his wife found him showering kisses on their daughter, a child of four, and noticed his brimming eyes. She was startled and asked what was wrong.

"Nothing, nothing."

It was, in fact, fear of the future and a horror of poverty. But hope was easily restored. The idea that better days were yet to come consoled him enough to struggle on. He was thirty-four, it was the beginning of his career: all beginnings were difficult. So he worked, waited, spent, asked for credit or borrowed, barely paying it back, and in an untimely fashion.

That day's pressing debt was the damned four hundred and something *mil-reis* for carriage hire. Never had a bill remained unsettled for so long, nor grown as much as this one; and, granted, the creditor had not held a knife to his chest, but that day his words had been harsh, and his gestures rude, and Honório wanted to settle up at once. It was five o'clock in the afternoon. He'd remembered to go to a moneylender, but had turned back without daring to ask for a thing. It was entering the Rua da Assembléia that he saw the wallet on the ground, picked it up, put it in his pocket, and walked on.

For the first few minutes Honório thought of nothing; he walked on, and on, and on as far as Largo da Carioca. He stopped in the square for a few moments before turning into Rua da Carioca, but quickly turned back and headed into Rua Uruguaiana. Without realizing it, he soon found himself in Largo de São Francisco de Paula; and again, without realizing it, went into a café. He ordered something and leaned against the wall, gazing outside. He was afraid to open the wallet; perhaps he would find nothing in it, just papers of no value to him. At the same time, and this was the main cause of his reflections, his conscience was inquiring if he would be capable of using the money he might find there. It was not questioning him with the air of one who does not know the answer, but with a rather ironic, censorious tone. Could he use the money to pay his debt? That was the point. His conscience finally told him he couldn't, that he should hand the wallet in to the police, or put word out, but no sooner had it told him this than he remembered his dire situation, which tugged at him and urged him to go pay the carriage company. His thoughts went as far as to tell him that had he been the one to lose the wallet, no one would have handed it in, an insinuation that heartened him.

All this before he'd even opened the wallet. He finally took it from his pocket, but fearfully, almost clandestinely; he opened it, trembling. There was money in it, a lot of money. He didn't count it, but he saw two notes of two hundred, a few fifties, and twenties. He calculated there were about seven hundred *mil-reis* or more; six hundred at the very least. It was his debt paid and a few less pressing expenses. Honório was tempted to ignore his conscience, run to the carriage company, pay, and, when the debt was settled, bid the whole thing goodbye; then he'd make peace with his conscience. He closed the wallet, and afraid of losing it, put it safely back in his pocket.

But he soon took it out again, and opened it, wanting to count the money. Count it for what? Was it his? In the end he convinced himself and counted it. There were seven hundred and thirty *mil-reis*. A shiver ran down Honório's spine. No one had seen him, no one knew. It might have been the hand of fortune, his lucky day, an angel . . . Honório was sorry he didn't believe in angels . . . But why shouldn't he believe in them? And he returned to the money, gazed at it, flicked through it; then he decided quite the opposite, not to use what he'd found, to give it back. Give it back to whom? He had a look to see if there was any identification in the wallet.

"If there's a name, any indication at all, I can't use the money," he thought.

He examined each of the wallet's compartments. He found letters, which he didn't open, folded notes, which he didn't read, and finally a calling card. He read the name; it was Gustavo's. So the wallet . . . ? He checked the outside and it did look like his friend's. He looked inside again and found two more cards, three more, five more. There was no doubt; it was his.

The discovery saddened him. He couldn't keep the money without doing something illicit and, in this case, painful to his own heart, for it would harm a friend. The whole castle he'd built came tumbling down, as if it were made of cards. He drank the last of his coffee, without noticing that it was cold. He left, and only then did he realize that it was almost dark. He headed home. Necessity seemed to press upon him once or twice, but he resisted.

"Be patient," he told himself, "I'll see what I can do tomorrow."

When he got home, he found Gustavo already there, somewhat preoccupied, and Amélia herself seemed so

too. He walked in laughing, and inquired if his friend was
missing anything.

"No."

"Nothing?"

"Why?"

"Put your hand in your pocket. Is anything missing?"

"My wallet's missing," said Gustavo, without putting
his hand in his pocket. "Do you know if anyone has found
it?"

"I found it," said Honório, handing it to him.

Gustavo snatched it and looked suspiciously at his
friend. His look was a stab in Honório's heart; after all
that battle with necessity, it was a sad reward. He smiled
bitterly, and, since his friend had asked, explained exactly
where he'd found it.

"But did you recognize it?"

"No, I found your calling cards."

Honório turned around and went to change for dinner. Then Gustavo took out his wallet again, opened it,
looked in a compartment, took out one of the notes his
friend hadn't even bothered to open or read, and handed
it to an anxious, trembling Amélia, who tore it into thirty
thousand pieces. It was a love letter.

Translated by Lynne Reay Pereira and Alison Entrekin

Account of the Incident

Rubem Fonseca

EARLY IN THE MORNING on May 3, a brown cow was crossing the bridge over the Coroado River, at marker 53, in the direction of Rio de Janeiro.

A passenger bus of the Única Auto Ônibus firm, license plates RF-80-07-83 and JR-81-12-27, was crossing the Coroado bridge in the direction of São Paulo.

When he saw the cow, the driver, Plínio Sérgio, tried

Born in 1925, RUBEM FONSECA has been a dominant figure in Brazilian literature for over four decades. He has won the Juan Rulfo Prize, considered Latin America's Nobel Prize, and the Jabuti Prize, Brazil's highest literary honor. His setting is frequently Rio de Janeiro, his home since the age of eight. Two collections of stark, wholly unsentimental short stories, *Feliz ano novo* (*Happy New Year*) and *O cobrador* (*The Taker*), firmly established him in both popular and critical circles as a master of the realistic narrative of urban violence and anomie. His first collection of short stories in English, *The Taker and Other Stories*, appeared in 2008. Although the setting of this story is outside the city, its violence is subdued, and its characters are rural; his identification with the poor and his implicit indignation at social injustice resonate clearly.

---

to avoid hitting it. He collided with the cow, hit the side of the bridge, and the bus plunged into the river.

On the bridge, the cow was dead.

Under the bridge, the dead were: a woman dressed in a long skirt and yellow blouse, appearing to be about 20, who would never be identified; Ovídia Monteiro, 34 years old; Manuel dos Santos Pinhal, a 35-year-old Portuguese whose papers identified him as a member of the Beverage Manufacturing Employees Union; the child Reinaldo, age one year, Manuel's son; Eduardo Varela, married, 43 years old.

The accident was witnessed by Elias Gentil dos Santos and his wife Lucília, residents in the vicinity. Elias tells his wife to fetch a large knife from home. "A knife?" Lucília asks. "A knife, quick, you idiot," says Elias. He is worried. Ah! Lucília understands. Lucília leaves, running.

Marcílio da Conceição appears. Elias looks at him with hatred. Ivonildo de Moura Júnior also appears. And that fool hasn't brought the knife! thinks Elias. He is angry at everyone; his hands tremble. Elias spits on the ground several times, strongly, until his mouth is dry.

"Hello, Mr. Elias," says Marcílio.

"Hello," says Elias between clenched teeth, looking to the sides. That mulatto! thinks Elias.

"It's really something," says Ivonildo, leaning on the bridge railing and looking at the firefighters and police below.

On the bridge, besides the driver of a car from the Highway Patrol, there are only Elias, Marcílio, and Ivonildo.

"Situation ain't goin' too good," says Elias, looking at the cow.

He can't take his eyes off the cow.

"That's true," says Marcílio.

The three men look at the cow.

In the distance they see Lucília, running toward them.

Elias spits again. "If I could, I'd be rich too," says Elias.

Marcílio and Ivonildo nod their heads, look at the cow and at Lucília, who approaches in a run. Lucília is also displeased to see the two men.

"Good morning, Dona Lucília," says Marcílio.

Lucília responds with a nod of her head. "Did I take a long time?" she asks her husband, panting.

Elias takes the knife in his hand, as if it were a dagger; he looks with hatred at Marcílio and Ivonildo. He spits on the ground. He leaps onto the cow.

"The filet's in the rear," says Lucília.

Elias cuts up the cow.

Marcílio approaches. "Will you lend me your knife afterwards, Mr. Elias?"

"No," Elias replies.

Marcílio withdraws, moving quickly. Ivonildo runs at top speed.

"They're going to get knives," says Elias angrily, "that mulatto, that sonofabitch." His hands, his shirt, and his pants are soaked in blood. "You should've brought a bag, a sack, two sacks, you imbecile. Go get a couple of sacks," Elias orders.

Lucília dashes away.

Elias has already cut off two large chunks of meat when, running, Marcílio and his wife Dalva, Ivonildo and his mother-in-law Aurélia, and Erandir Medrado and his brother Valfrido Medrado appear. All are carrying knives and machetes. They attack the cow.

Lucília reappears, running. She can hardly speak. She is eight months pregnant, suffers from worms, and her house is on top of a hill, and the bridge at the top of another hill. Lucília has brought a second knife with her. Lucília cuts into the cow.

"Somebody lend me a knife or I'll arrest all of you," says the driver of the patrol car. The Medrado brothers, who have brought several knives, lend one to the driver.

Carrying a saw, a machete, and a small axe, João Leitão, the butcher, appears, accompanied by two helpers.

"You can't," shouts Elias.

João Leitão kneels down near the cow.

"You can't," says Elias, shoving João. João falls down.

"You can't," the Medrado brothers shout.

"You can't," shouts everyone except the police driver.

João moves away; ten yards off, he stops, with his helpers, and watches.

Half the cow's flesh has been removed. It wasn't easy to cut off the tail. No one succeeded in cutting off the head and hooves. The guts no one wanted.

Elias has filled two sacks. The other men use their shirts as if they were sacks.

First to leave are Elias and his wife. "Cook me up a thick steak," he tells Lucília, smiling.

"I'm going to ask Dona Dalva for some potatoes, I'm going to make you French fries too," replies Lucília.

The remains of the cow lie in a pool of blood. João whistles to one of his two helpers. One of them brings a wheelbarrow. The remains of the cow are placed in the wheelbarrow. On the bridge nothing is left but the pool of blood.

Translated by Clifford Landers

Altitude

Adriana Lisboa

GOING UP THE MOUNTAIN by bus is different. Going
up the mountain by bus, at night, is different. And if it's
a winter night, and you take a seat by the window with
nobody next to you, and if nobody on the bus talks and
you only hear the soft groan of the motor (new bus), and
if there's no fog, and if in your chest there's something like

---

ADRIANA LISBOA was born in 1970 in Rio de Janeiro. She
was a flautist and vocalist before dedicating herself to writing
and translation. Upon publication of *Os fios da memória* (*Threads
of Memory*) in 1999, she was acclaimed as among the most
distinctive voices of a new generation of Brazilian novelists.
The pieces here are from *Caligrafias*, a collection of what she
calls "little narratives." Somewhere between prose-poetry and
micro-fiction, and evoking the Zen sensibility of the classical
haiku poet and travel diarist, Bashō, these miniatures explore
the intimate emotional resonance of a moment in place, or, in
these cases, three distinct places: the canyon-lands of Goiás; the
dizzying ascent between coastal Rio and the jagged, jungle covered mountains known as the Organ Pipe Range and Brasília,
the high modernist national capital.

---

a piano playing Chopin on its own, then everything is so different that it's almost as if the world had been created something like twenty-four hours ago.

Someone told you that yesterday they went out and only got home at five in the morning and slept until one in the afternoon and ate spaghetti with sausages and ground beef for lunch. Someone taught you to say *konnichi wa*, a greeting in Japanese. Someone looked at you with kindness, someone else with curiosity (you were probably biting your lip and making faces as you read, on the subway), a taxi driver looked at you with a bit of ill will because the trip was a short one. Someone looked at you more insistently, with a dangerous look, and you almost succumbed.

And now you're going up the mountain by bus and your soul is made of spaghetti with sausages and the subway and a book and *konnichi wa*. Going up the mountain by bus is different. At night. The sky is black with many, so many stars scattered about, the trees are gray and sometimes they pass right up against the windows of the bus. On one stretch they disappear completely and you see the cities down below, clumps of lights that look like controlled fires, and the immense fire (uncontrollable but pacified) of the largest of them all, Rio, in a horizontal and shining strip, from where you departed on the nine o'clock bus.

Suddenly you ask yourself how many meters up you are, how many kilometers away. But what does it matter, if the world is twenty-four hours old, and if it is here, in this space between, that everything happens.

Translated by Malcolm K. McNee

The Dead Man in the Sea at Urca

Clarice Lispector

I WAS AT THE APARTMENT of Dona Lourdes, my
seamstress, trying on a new dress designed by Olly, and
Dona Lourdes said:

"A man drowned in the sea, look at the firemen."

I looked and only saw the sea, which must have been
very salty; blue sea, white houses. And the dead man?

CLARICE LISPECTOR (1925-1977) has gained an international reputation as perhaps Brazil's greatest modern stylist
after Guimarães Rosa. When Hélène Cixous, the foremost
French feminist literary critic, paid homage to Lispector in
her book *Reading with Clarice Lispector* (1990), it assured her
recognition as one of the premiere Latin American writers
of this century. Her work is well known in Europe and most
of her short stories, *crónicas*, and novels have appeared in the
United States, including *Near to the Wild Heart*, *Family Ties*,
The Foreign Legion, *The Stream of Life*, *The Hour of the Star*, and
Soulstorm (from which both stories in this collection are taken).
Fundamentally a poet writing in prose, she mixes subjectivity
and objectivity, spontaneity and detachment, sentiment and
irony, to reveal the precious smallness of our shared humanity.

The dead man pickled in brine. I don't want to die! I screamed to myself, silent there in my dress. The dress is yellow and blue. And I? Dying of heat, not dying of a blue sea.

I'll tell you a secret: my dress is beautiful, and I don't want to die. On Friday the dress will be at home, and on Saturday I'll wear it. Without death, just blue sea. Do yellow clouds exist? Golden ones do. I have no story. Does the dead man? He does: he went to take a swim in the sea at Urca, the fool, and he died—who told him to go? I'm careful when I bathe in the sea, I'm no fool, and I only go to Urca to try on a new dress. And three blouses. S. went with me. She is most particular at a fitting. And the dead man? Particularly dead?

I'll tell you a story: Once upon a time there was a young fellow who liked to swim in the sea. So, one Wednesday morning he went to Urca. I don't go to Urca, to the rocks of Urca, because it's full of rats. But the young man didn't pay any attention to the rats. Nor did the rats pay any attention to him. Urca's cluster of white houses. That he noticed. And then there was a woman trying on a dress, who arrived too late—the young man was already dead. Briny. Were there piranhas in the sea? I pretended not to understand. I don't, in fact, understand death. A boy, dead?

Dead like the fool he was. One should only go to Urca to try on a joyful dress. The woman, who is me, only wants gaiety. But I bow down before death. That will come, will come, will come. When? Ah, that's just it, it can come at any moment. But I, who was trying on a dress in the heat of the morning, asked God for a sign. And I felt something so intense, an overwhelming scent of roses. So, I had my proof, in two tests: of God and of my dress.

One should only die a natural death, never in an accident, never drowned in the sea. I beg protection for my own, who are many. And the protection, I am sure, will come.

But what of the young man? And his story? He might have been a student. I will never know. I simply stood staring out at the sea and the cluster of houses. Dona Lourdes, imperturbable, asked if she should take it in at the waist a bit more. I said yes, a waistline is there to be seen tight. But I was in shock. In shock in my beautiful new dress.

Translated by Alexis Levitin

Plaza Mauá

Clarice Lispector

THE CABARET ON PLAZA MAUÁ was called The Erotica. And Luisa's stage name was Carla.

Carla was a dancer at The Erotica. She was married to Joaquim, who was killing himself working as a carpenter. And Carla "worked" at two jobs: dancing half nude and cheating on her husband.

Carla was beautiful. She had little teeth and a tiny waist. She was delicate throughout. She had scarcely any breasts, but she had well-shaped hips. She took an hour to make herself up; afterward, she seemed a porcelain doll. She was thirty but looked much younger.

There were no children. Joaquim and she couldn't get together. He worked until ten at night. She began work at exactly ten. She slept all day long.

Carla was a lazy Luisa. Arriving at night, when the time came to present herself to the public, she would begin to yawn, wishing she were in her nightgown in bed. This was also due to shyness. Incredible as it might

For Lispector's biographical information, see page 18.

seem, Carla was a timid Luisa. She stripped, yes, but the first moments of the dance, of voluptuous motion, were moments of shame. She only "warmed up" a few minutes later. Then she unfolded, she undulated, she gave all of herself. She was best at the samba. But a nice, romantic blues also turned her on.

She was asked to drink with the clients. She received a commission per bottle. She always chose the most expensive drinks. And she pretended to drink, but hers wasn't alcohol. The idea was to get the clients drunk and make them spend. It was boring talking with them. They would caress her, passing their hands over her tiny breasts. And she in a scintillating bikini. Beautiful.

Once in a while she would sleep with a client. She would take the money, keep it well hidden in her bra, and the next day she would buy some new clothes. She had clothes without end. She bought blue jeans. And necklaces. A pile of necklaces. And bracelets, and rings.

Sometimes, just for variety's sake, she danced in blue jeans and without a bra, her breasts swinging among the flashing necklaces. She wore bangs and, using a black pencil, painted on a beauty mark close to her delicate lips. It was adorable. She wore long pendant earrings, sometimes pearl, sometimes imitation gold.

In moments of unhappiness, she turned to Celsinho, a man who wasn't a man. They understood each other well. She told him her troubles, complained about Joaquim, complained about inflation. Celsinho, a successful transvestite, listened to it all and gave her advice. They weren't rivals. They each worked their own turf.

Celsinho came from the nobility. He had given up

everything to follow his vocation. He didn't dance. But he did wear lipstick and false eyelashes. The sailors of Plaza Mauá loved him. And he played hard to get. He only gave in at the very end. And he was paid in dollars. After changing the money on the black market, he invested it in the Banco Halles. He was very afraid of growing old, destitute and forsaken. Especially since an old transvestite is a sad thing. He took two envelopes of powdered proteins a day for energy. He had large hips and, from taking so many hormones, he had acquired a facsimile of breasts. Celsinho's stage name was Moleirão.

Moleirão and Carla brought good money to the owner of The Erotica. The smoke-filled atmosphere, the smell of alcohol. And the dance floor. It was tough being forced to dance with a drunken sailor. But what could you do. Everyone has his *métier*.

Celsinho had adopted a little girl of four. He was a real mother to her. He slept very little in order to look after the girl. And she lacked for nothing: she had only the best. Even a Portuguese nanny. On Sundays Celsinho took little Clareta to the zoo at the Quinta de Boa Vista. And they both ate popcorn. And they fed the monkeys. Little Clareta was afraid of the elephants. She asked: "Why do they have such big noses?"

Celsinho then told her a fantastic tale involving good fairies and bad fairies. Or else he would take her to the circus. And they would suck hard, clicking candies, the two of them. Celsinho wanted a brilliant future for little Clareta: marriage with a man of fortune, children, jewels.

Carla had a Siamese cat who looked at her with hard blue eyes. But Carla scarcely had time to take care of the creature: either she was sleeping, or dancing, or out shopping. The cat was named Leleu. And it drank milk with its delicate little red tongue.

Joaquim hardly saw Luisa. He refused to call her Carla. Joaquim was fat and short, of Italian descent. It had been a Portuguese woman neighbor who had given him the name Joaquim. His name was Joaquim Fioriti. Fioriti? There was nothing flowerlike about him.

The maid who worked for Joaquim and Luisa was a wily black woman who stole whatever she could. Luisa hardly ate, in order to keep her figure. Joaquim drowned himself in minestrone. The maid knew about everything, but kept her mouth shut. It was her job to polish Carla's jewelry with Brasso and Silvo. When Joaquim was sleeping and Carla working, this maid, by the name of Silvinha, wore her mistress's jewelry. And she was kind of grayish-black in color.

This is how what happened happened.

Carla was confiding in Moleirão when she was asked to dance by a tall man with broad shoulders. Celsinho lusted after him. And he ate his heart out in envy. He was vindictive.

When the dance ended and Carla returned to sit down next to Moleirão, he could hardly hold in his rage. And Carla, innocent. It wasn't her fault she was attractive. And, in fact, the big man appealed to her. She said to Celsinho:

"I'd go to bed with that one for free."

Celsinho said nothing. It was almost three in the morning. The Erotica was full of men and women. Many mothers and housewives went there for the fun of it and to earn a bit of pocket money.

Then Carla said, "It's so good to dance with a real man."

Celsinho sprang, "But you're not a real woman!"

"Me? How come I'm not?" said the startled girl, who, dressed that night in black, in a long dress with long sleeves, looked like a nun. She did this on purpose to excite those men who desired a pure woman.

"You," screamed Celsinho, "are no woman at all! You don't even know how to fry an egg! And I do! I do! I do!"

Carla turned into Luisa. White, bewildered. She had been struck in her most intimate femininity. Confused, staring at Celsinho who had the face of a witch.

Carla didn't say a word. She stood up, crushed her cigarette in the ashtray, and, without turning to anyone, abandoning the party at its height, she left.

On foot, in black, on the Praça Mauá at three in the morning. Like the lowest of whores. Alone. Without recourse. It was true: she didn't know how to fry an egg. And Celsinho was more of a woman than she.

The plaza was dark. And Luisa breathed deeply. She looked at the lampposts. The plaza was empty.

And in the sky, the stars.

Translated by Alexis Levitin

The Traffic Light

Helena Parente Cunha

EIGHT IN THE MORNING. At the corner of Bento Lisboa Street and Plaza Machado. The traffic light, the sun turned on, the sky turned off. The bus, the cars, the pushcarts, pedestrians, stones and asphalt, the pigeons. A dense foliage heavy with carbon monoxide stretches out across the electric wires. The open doors, the closed doors, windows in the process of being opened or closed. Apartments and hotel rooms. The hotel. On the brink of the sidewalk's edge, a couple standing moving. A smile and a

HELENA PARENTE CUNHA was born in Salvador, Bahia in 1929. She lives in Rio de Janeiro, where she was a Professor of Literary Theory at the Universidade Federal. She published several volumes of poetry and short stories before writing her first and best-known novel, *Mulher no espelho* (1983), in which she plays with the notions of character, closure, and unified perspective while exploring the issue of female identity. It won the Premio Cruz e Sousa Prize and established her as an international literary figure when it was translated into English as *Woman between Mirrors* (1989) by Fred P. Ellison and Naomi Lindstrom.

sigh. Trucks, bicycles, motorcycles, exhaust fumes. Stores
opening, a racket of metal and rubber. The wheels and the
feet. The pigeons' wings. A pollution of flapping wings.
On the brink of the sidewalk's edge, the couple sketching
themselves in. The scream of gestures. Fat and bald, sparse
white hair. Him, tubby. Her, dark and sinuous, reflections
from the sea in her brown hair. Tenuous. The red stop-
light. Smile. Sigh. His. Hers. Horns, braking, pigeons
cooing. Wearing jacket and tie, he holds his leather wallet
and licks with his fingers one bill and then another. In
her silvery mesh dress, she wraps around her fingers the
strands of her pearl necklace, not hiding the two beads
whose pearly coating has flaked off. The fruit juice stand
restarts its colors. The oily wind pushes its way through the
crammed-together voices and the close-shut mouths and
the pollution-specked mirrors of the vehicles. At the brink
of the sidewalk's edge, the couple standing there doesn't
see the succession of movement slipping by. He puts the
billfold away in the pocket of his striped jacket. Fleshy.
She puts the money away in the plastic purse the color
of silvery mesh fabric. Wispy. The roar of gestures. The
bus, the cars, the vans, bicycles, motorcycles, pedophiles,
panhandlers, pebbles, imprecations, sequences, pigeons,
dissidences. The speedy asphalt. The traffic light. A lustful
smile, he grabs her arm. Not to be delayed, she sighs, trying to cross the street. The couple is in movement, in the
movement of the concrete, full morning of 1 minute past
8. A greasy smile. A sigh from the bottom of a well. She
wants. He wants. To go. To stay. She and he counterpoised
in the crossroads. Red light. He passes his hand over the
fragile shoulder and brings the sinuous body toward the

arc of his belly. The horns, the motors, the birds in movement. She tries to get free of the round belly, break out in
the green opening of the light. Greasy, he tries to stop the
attempted stepping free. Impenetrable, she halts. The yellow taxi halts, the leaves halt in the wind's coming to a halt.
At the brink of the sidewalk's edge, the fat-filled morning doesn't halt. Her. Him. Kissing her neck and mouth,
slobbering over the curves. Viscous. Brunette, swift hair,
with reflections of the morning sea. A bubbling of muffled
frothing sea. The sparse strands of white hair don't com-
mingle with the deep browns from the depths of the sea.
In its plastic sandal with bits of colored glass, the slender
foot goes into the gravel at the curb. The hairy hand grasps
the delicate arm, an ambulance pulls out of the hospital,
a pigeon falls dead in the intersection. Wheels and shod
feet, brakes and bare feet, and exhaust fumes, he won't let
the girl cross. A smile of satisfaction at a night (un)slept
in a cheap hotel room. The sticky grazing of a mouth on
the breath of hair slipping out loose. A fresh wind doesn't
raise the hem of the clinging silver mesh dress. It's her
leg that's showing. Fresh flower stalk. It's his hand that's
starting in again. Thick octopus. Rolling along, motors,
feet on the asphalt, feet on pedals, feet on the edge of the
sidewalk, it's 3 minutes past 8 o'clock in the blur of the
morning. Her trying to get away, with the green light.
Him trying to stretch out a red light. The fruit juice stand
draws in the hot colors of the fruits. Two girls in school
uniforms cross the street with their books hanging from
their hands and a flower twined in their hair. The man of
suet and grease wants to grab hold and hold on. The girl
water and muffled sea foam wants to break free. 3 minutes
17 seconds past 8. A Mercedes and a Beetle pull up beside

each other, the drivers challenge each other, sharing their anxiety to hit the accelerator, together at the red light. A boy with torn trousers passes slowly and looks quickly at the pastry at the snack bar. The girl with reflections from the sea doesn't sigh and doesn't breathe. The man with the circling belly slithers in. The stones past the sidewalk's edge sharpen their knives and their barbed wire. The noises of the compressed morning. It's 4 minutes past 8. Horns piercing the hour, motors belching out poison, blenders slashing fruit to a mutilated pulp, you can't hear the polluted flapping of the pigeons' wings. Two feathers fall onto the gravel at the curb. An entire strip of road is holding the morning in its clutches at the exact same hour. At the brink of the sidewalk's edge, a man and a woman are moving in search of new movements. The bellowing of gestures. He raises his hand in the direction of the fruit juice stand. She wags her hand no. Green light. Red light. 5 minutes and 10 seconds past 8. Light. Light. Green. Red. A lustful look on his face. A crinkling wave of disgust spread across her face. A woman smiles and buys a pastry for the child with the torn trousers. Many faces passing, stopping, passing without stopping, not smiling, one after another. Gravitations and wheels and weights and feet and the blades of the juice blenders. Knives. A panhandler goes by with a live pigeon in his hand. The fat bald man moves his hand to his crotch and grabs hold of his sex through his pants and through his eyes gives a honeyed smile. The girl her body a flower stalk bathed in the sea tries to break off, in her mouth, with its red lipstick, the unleashed urge to vomit. He grips his sex harder, his smile more honeyed, 6 minutes past 8, the look in his eyes oilier. The interminable hour laden with carbon monoxide drags along in the tense wind. 6 minutes and 11 indispensable seconds past 8. The girl doesn't vomit. The light changes. The girl doesn't see the light. The girl of the sea grottoes breaks away from the octopus and leaps over the barbed wire and knife blade at the edge of the sidewalk. The fat arm trapped out there in the hard air tries to hold back her urge to tear away. The roaring of the gesture. A noise of brakes and tires and soles of shoes and soles of bare feet on the asphalt and on the stones of the sidewalk. And shouts. And voices. And car doors opening and thunderous horns and the pigeons flying higher and the pastry falling out of the mouth of the child with the torn trousers. The oily man doesn't budge, his hand walled up into the worn-out space. A lighthearted wind ruffles the meager strands on the bald head. A trail of blood reaches out to the gravel at the curb. Between the feet writhing near the body spread loose on the asphalt, rolls the high-heeled sandal with its clasp of little stones of colored glass. A sudden man throws himself on the silvery plastic purse and runs off, pushing aside person and people, forward and back. From inside the purse two little identification photos fall out onto the roughness of the asphalt. A boy about five years old. A woman about eighty. The waves of the pool of blood shine in the sunlight. A noise of voices and of soles of shoes and of soles of feet and of blenders and of wheels and of little pigeons and of motors burning fuel and of pollution particles and of the endless stone-grinding machine in the measured composition of the blades and knives. 7 minutes 19 seconds past 8 on the morning of tar. Light and lights.

Translated by Naomi Lindstrom

Josete Killed Herself

Sonia Coutinho

I WALK TO THE KITCHEN CABINET, and pour myself another whiskey. I put a Billie Holliday album on the stereo, lie down on the couch, and light up a menthol cigarette. I'm very tired. Tonight I was at the newspaper until almost midnight, even though it's Sunday. But, close to the time for the final wrap, a really poorly written story, about twelve pages long, landed in my hands. Five

SONIA COUTINHO, award-winning novelist and short story writer, has been hailed as one of the most innovative female authors in contemporary Brazil. She was born in 1939 in a small town in the state of Bahia, grew up in Salvador, and in 1968, moved to Rio de Janeiro, where she currently resides. Her fiction focuses on middle-class female protagonists and their struggle to achieve independence and self-fulfillment. She has published seven collections of short stories, four novels, and a novella for young adults. Also translated into German, Polish, French, and Spanish, her stories have appeared in *Ploughshares*, *Michigan Quarterly Review*, *Beacons—A Journal of Literary Translation*, and *Brasil/Brazil*. This story is from *O último verão de Copacabana* (*Last Summer in Copacabana*).

people were kidnapped and killed in Pavuna and in Nova Iguaçu. A couple had been handcuffed and burned inside a Chevrolet Opala. The photos made you want to throw up. A guy named Carlinhos Neguinho survived the massacre, and because his cousin had been killed, he decided to tell everything he knew.

I had to rewrite it on an old typewriter. The ribbon spool fell off and the keys were coming loose, while the managing editor stared at me in a fury: I was holding up the final wrap. I was sweating all over, and when I left I had this need to see someone. I called Carla, but she wasn't up to it; I just came straight home.

Home to this dirty, empty apartment, where about fifteen minutes ago the phone rang. It was Cigarrinho, the gofer at the newspaper, to give me the news: redheaded Josete had just died. She had been in critical condition in the ICU of Miguel Couto Hospital for a week, after an attempted suicide with Diazepam and gas. She swallowed the pills and stuck her head in the oven with the gas on, in her small and lonely apartment in Copacabana's Posto Seis neighborhood.

I stretch out on the couch now, rest my aching head on a pillow, and all at once I see various images of Josete: her faded jeans, her vests from India, and her suede purse with fringes; the stories she would tell when she returned from some hot assignment; the way she would hold a cigarette between her fingers, pacing back and forth in the large smoke-filled newsroom, her pretty face looking troubled, her gaze distant; and that slender, perfect body of a thirty-year-old woman, her sensual gestures like those of a whore.

There are a million stories about her. People say the entire editorial staff slept with Josete; she didn't always know who she'd had sex with the day before. "I wonder if it was Claudio last night?" she supposedly asked one day. "I hope it wasn't Claudio, I find him gross."

Now that she's dead, the sadder side of her story will emerge: that she had lost her parents while still a child in that small country town where she was born. She was left with a trust fund, a permanent feeling of irremediable loss, and the impression that her father had killed her mother. It was he who had invited her on that trip when the airplane crashed.

Journalism is a hard profession, especially for someone who, like me, is over forty, an age when copyeditors begin to drink more than they should. Or for a woman: today, Arlette, bleached hair and a little drunk, sat next to me, writing a story about a boy, an adopted child, who was tortured by his stepmother. The neighbors reported the abuse and the police went to check. The policemen came down hard on her. One of them punched the woman in the face and knocked out one of her front teeth. Later I edited the story and wrote the caption for a picture that shows the woman, toothless and in her blood-spattered clothes, arriving at the police station to make a statement.

"Shit! Damn it!" Arlette exclaimed as she wrote. "I can't take this any longer! The newspaper is a cesspool; it destroys a woman's skin and her soul. It squeezes the life out of us, it grinds us down. One of these days, I'm getting out of here."

But, Arlette, I suspect that you'll stay. We'll both die fighting; there'll be no truce. As much as you think of leaving, you won't, and neither will I. And if you do, sooner or later you'll come back. This is our world, the circus that is our life, the show that must go on. We come to that newsroom from all over the country, each for a different reason: it's our Foreign Legion. We wouldn't know how to live any other way.

"Do you realize what a complex machine this is?" Maciel asked me the other day. "It's as if we wrote a book every day. Each day's newspaper is the size of a book, created by all our heads thinking together."

Maciel comes from a small town in the state of Santa Catarina, and has had many jobs: he was a store clerk, a book salesman, and even a racecar driver, before becoming a reporter. He's been working in the profession for ten years, and has his own philosophy about it:

"I don't get worked up, you know what I mean? All I need is to find the right person to question. I mean, the people who can really give me information. There's no point in running around; you have to keep your cool. Actually, the facts repeat themselves, and all the stiffs look alike. Fires, car accidents, robberies—it doesn't change much. We already know the procedure to follow in each case. We talk to a witness, to the business owner, to the driver, etc."

At first I thought the best reporter was González, maybe because he was from Argentina and had an imposing physique: he was tall, strong, tanned, and had gray hair. But folks told me he was just a hot reporter who knew, for example, how to dress like a biker and infiltrate a gang of drug dealers to gather information for a story. And that the best one may be Renato, whose father is a

Spanish Basque and whose mother is from Calabria, but he was born in Alagoas. He looks and speaks more like an *Alagoano*, and is always talking about politics.

"Now I know less and less about anything," Renato says. "I've been a little mixed -up. I'm still accepted among leftist groups, but people consider me a moderate. I've had lots of disappointments."

We all have disappointments, Renato; dreams that don't materialize or that we're unable to fulfill. Mine was to write a novelistic report on Copacabana. About ten years ago I wrote the first paragraph; I still have it memorized:

"In Copacabana there are no dramatic sunsets. The light turns less intense and more diffuse; it dims gently along the beach, blending in with the white salt dust. And as darkness descends gently, the buildings in profile lose their colors, and thousands of windows transform into countless small, illuminated squares."

Copacabana: the dream of every young person from the interior, fulfilled at last; the walled-off rectangle of starless sky that I see from my window. My music is the squealing of a million tires; my perfume, the sweet-sour smoke from the cars' tailpipes.

"Nights in Copacabana bring a veiled threat, as if an immense eye were peering from behind the shadows, a huge, humid and malevolent eye fed by Maria Bethânia's voice, her coarse screams," I then wrote.

I wanted to tell the neighborhood's history, talk about Prado Júnior Street, the Alley of Hunger, pizza and beer, jogging on the beach early in the morning, the Yemanjá festivities, and the outdoor bars along Avenida Atlântica.

And I would listen to testimonials: a stripper, a snack bar owner, a boutique salesgirl. As well as a woman in her early forties, tanned from the beach, her hair dyed titian, strolling on the sidewalk with her toy poodle or tiny Pekingese.

Copacabana: an impressive preparation for the ruins of the year 3000, when it will have been declared a national monument to kitsch. Copacabana invaded by rats; Copacabana evacuated after an epidemic plague. A powerful thunderstorm causes a deluge in Copacabana. The water rises above the twelfth floor of every building, and even the tallest hotels merely stick out like half-submerged towers. A lightning bolt ignites a fire on the top floor of the Othon Hotel.

My two sisters, both of whom are from the interior of Bahia and deeply Catholic, find it strange that I haven't gotten married. They think I've lost all the emotions everyone considers "human and normal," because of the life I lead. Ridiculous, completely ridiculous. What a pain in the ass, to be tied forever to another person, to have to accept a forced coexistence. There's nothing more unnatural than marriage. My true family is there in that smoke-filled newsroom, where roses wither.

Billie Holliday stops singing, I turn off the stereo. My whiskey is finished but I don't pour another. I'm going to try to fall asleep, even though I suspect that again I'll wake up in fear, at that very same time—the Hour of the Wolf—when those who can, hear the very high and quiet sound of the Madmen's Carillon.

Apparently I was the only one at the newspaper who didn't go to bed with Josete. I'm addicted to Carla, who

carries extra appendages in the front part of her body—
she's the star at the Alaska Gallery drag shows. But I find
some consolation in thinking that Josete, of course, was
frigid. She was a collective victim, a child rejected a thousand times, a sacred object for all to manipulate or ingest:
God's blood, a ticket to Resurrection.

Unable to feel pleasure, Josete searched in vain, in each
relationship, for an affection that was never there. She
killed herself because of her frigidity; she no longer was
able to go to bed with her rejecting father, the one who
had led her mother to her death. Cigarrinho's phone call
was like the final touch, and the statue of Josete is now
ready: she's dead.

And now, suddenly, she invades the living room of
this empty and dirty apartment, her immense, fluid body
expanding and taking over the entire space, her feet protruding out through the window. Her red hair, like the
hair of her double, Ann Margret, floats in space, spreading the sweet smell of cigarettes and typographer's lead
that impregnates all of us forever. Her jeans are soiled,
but her tight see-through top is still unsullied, revealing
her small, childish breasts, which I touch, in a completely
asexual caress.

Translated by Cristina Ferreira-Pinto Bailey

Ipanema Is a Long Way from Home

Paula Parisot

MANY HAVE HEARD of or even visited Ipanema's beaches, Copacabana, Leblon, Sugar Loaf Mountain, Corcovado, Maracanã Stadium, Rio's Botanical Gardens, the Tijuca Forest and the Rodrigo de Freitas Lagoon. But few know that this area of the city admired for its natural beauty and home of Rio's most affluent citizens, is just one municipality of seventeen that comprise the Metropolitan Region of Rio de Janeiro, also known as Grande Rio. Of all of them, the most densely populated and the wealthi-

PAULA PARISOT was born in Rio de Janeiro. After earning a degree in Industrial Design, she was awarded a scholarship to continue her studies at the New School in New York, where she received her M.F.A. Her first book of short stories, *A dama da solidão* (*The Lady of Solitude*), has been translated into Spanish, and one of the stories appeared in the online magazine *Words Without Borders*. Her novel *Gonzos e parafusos* (*Hinges and Screws*) was published concurrently with this collection. She currently lives in São Paulo. "Ipanema Is a Long Way from Home" was written especially for this anthology.

est is Rio itself, with more than six million inhabitants. The total population of Grande Rio is over twelve million people. The three municipalities of São Gonçalo, Duque de Caxias and Nova Iguaçú each have about a million inhabitants, most of them of lower socioeconomic status.

Gisele was born twenty years ago in the Nova Aurora neighborhood in Belford Roxo, a slightly smaller municipality with approximately five hundred thousand inhabitants. She is the daughter of a mulata mother and a white father, who left when Gisele was just a child. Her mother, Maria da Graça, raised the girl working as a nail tech in a modest beauty salon near her house. She insisted that her daughter study in the biggest local public school, Colégio Estadual Bom Pastor. She did not want her daughter to grow up illiterate as she was. Gisele was very studious and her dream was to become a doctor.

In the meantime, because of their economic difficulties, Gisele had to start work when she was sixteen. She found a job as a nanny in a wealthy home in Ipanema, in Rio's South Zone. To get to work at eight in Ipanema, Gisele got up at 4:00 am, since she had to take two buses after walking for about fifteen minutes to the bus stop.

It was still dark in Nova Aurora, but there were always other people waiting for the bus, which arrived nearly empty. Gisele sat next to the window; she liked to watch the sun rise, dissolving the darkness of the night. The bus would make its stops and more passengers boarded in Farula, Heliópolis and Andrade de Araújo. When they got to the Piam neighborhood, all the seats were taken. At this point some had to stand, but Gisele hardly noticed, as she watched the day dawning. Finally, the bus left the Belford Roxo municipality and merged on to the Via Dutra, the same highway that links the state of Rio de Janeiro with the state of São Paulo. Gisele observed that the sky was getting lighter and a kind of confidence in what the day would bring took over her thoughts. When the bus turned on to Avenida Brazil she saw the streetlights turning off.

The last stop was the railroad station, the Central do Brasil, where she picked up her second ride, a bus without air conditioning that cost half as much. She almost always had to stand, since the buses were jammed. Now she could no longer gaze at the landscape because of the number of people around her, but she noticed that they passed by Praça Quinze in the center of the city, the Flamengo waterfront with its view of the Bay of Guanabara, then Botafogo and finally Copacabana, where she could sit down until they reached Ipanema.

At eight AM on the dot she rang the doorbell of her employer's home. She was rarely late.

Gisele cared for the lady's little three-year-old girl and her employer grew fond of her and began to teach her etiquette, how to sit at the table and speak correctly, pointing out the small grammar errors that she made. Gisele paid close attention to how her employer dressed, gestured and talked on the telephone.

Maria da Graça noticed on the weekends when her daughter was home, that Gisele was different.

"You are just like one of those society girls from the South Zone, especially with those clothes that your employer gives you."

After working in this household for two years, the lady of the house had to dismiss her because her husband, an executive in a multinational company, was transferred overseas. She gave Gisele various presents, clothing, a television, and a bonus. Even though it was a reasonably large sum, the money went on dentures for her mother and a new roof for the house, since a leak was ruining the furniture. So it was not long before Gisele had to go back to work instead of returning to her studies, as she had planned.

Their house was simple, but Maria da Graça owned it and she insisted on surrounding it with a barbed wire fence. In the back there was a yard with a banana tree which had been planted when the house was built. In the beginning the house had just one room, where mother and daughter slept. The second room could only be built when Gisele started working as a nanny.

Gisele tried to find work near home but she was not successful. Since she needed a dependable salary, she agreed to work as a cashier in a supermarket in the Méier neighborhood, a traditional middle class district in Rio's North Zone. Even though it was closer than Ipanema, where she had worked as a nanny, it took almost as long to go from Belford Roxo to Méier. She took just one bus, the traffic was still terrible, and there were several traffic jams along the way due to the number of cars of all types that congested the roads. She almost always walked the rest of the way. The only thing that bothered her was the presence of certain men who took advantage of the crowd to rub up against and fondle the women. Especially pretty girls like her. Gisele protected herself with her bag. Normally the bus was so packed that she could not move. But because she was so often molested, Gisele decided, on her mother's advice, to wear a safety pin attached to her clothing.

Once when she was going home from work, a man approached Gisele from behind and pressed against her body.

"Please move back," Gisele said.

"The bus is too full, and if you don't like it, take a taxi, princess," said the guy, grasping her by the hips and rubbing up against her.

Without hesitating, Gisele took the pin attached to her blouse and stabbed the man in the thigh.

He jumped back and exclaimed, "What, are you crazy?" Then he backed off.

The supermarket was on Diaz da Cruz street, which was the busiest one in Méier. In a short time the manager of the store noticed Gisele was an excellent worker, she was never late, she did not make mistakes, she treated the customers professionally and she did not complain if they doubled her shift.

On Sundays, her only day off, she went to Ipanema beach, near where she had worked as a nanny. She followed the same route, taking two buses, however on weekends there was less traffic. The trip lasted just over three hours. She took an umbrella and applied sunblock, because she had inherited her father's white skin. Her dark wavy hair and her slender and well-proportioned body drew attention, but nevertheless she wore a discreet two-piece suit.

Gisele would sit near one of the volleyball nets. A tall blond boy began to take an interest in her. He noticed she was always alone, wearing the same blue bikini.

The boy asked his friends whether they knew the girl in the blue bikini who sat near the volleyball net. Nobody knew who she was. Gisele noticed that he would glance in her direction, sometimes their eyes would meet.

One day he approached her.

"My name is Henrique."

Gisele said nothing and just smiled.

"You come here every Sunday, don't you?"

"Yes."

There was a silence.

"You didn't tell me your name."

"Gisele."

Again they were at a loss for words.

"They're calling you," Gisele said.

Henrique turned around and one of his friends gestured to him saying, "Come on, we're going to start."

He felt like saying he wouldn't play this round but his team mates insisted, calling his name.

"You better go," she said with a smile.

That day Gisele's ride home went fast. She barely noticed the people around her, thinking about Henrique. The same occurred with him, instead of paying attention to the movie he went to with his friends, he was distracted by the memory of Gisele's sweet smile and the dimple in her chin.

From that day on they would always talk after the volleyball game. Henrique talked about movies, concerts, parties in Lapa and in the nightclubs of the South Zone. Since Gisele didn't see those films or go to those places, she answered that she studied a lot and did not have time for those things. So they talked about the temperature of the water, the people walking by and those stretched out under the sun or under beach umbrellas. Henrique brought mate or coconut milk for her, for which she thanked him. Sometimes she would blush at his courtesies and compliments. More than once he invited her to go to the movies, but Gisele always refused, saying that her mother was strict and she had to study because her college courses were difficult.

"What degree are you getting?"

"Medicine," answered Gisele, after a brief hesitation.

"I am doing industrial engineering at the Pontifical Catholic University. Where are you studying medicine?"

"Henrique, it's getting late, I have to go."

Gisele got up, tied her sarong around her waist, and folded the umbrella.

"Where do you live?"

"Nearby."

"Me too, I live on Aníbal de Mendonça street, and you?"

"On Nascimento Silva." She gave the street where she had worked as a nanny.

"May I walk you home?"

"No," said Gisele, impulsively. "That is, you don't need to, I have to stop by the store to buy a few things my mother needs. Thanks."

They said goodbye. When she got to the sidewalk she looked back and saw Henrique talking with some of his volleyball friends. She calmed down but even so she decided to walk for a few blocks in the direction away from Henrique's street to catch the bus.

The next day, the supermarket manager called Gisele to his office at the end of the day. He said that the chain was opening its first branch in the South Zone. It would be in Ipanema and he had selected her to work at the new store, which would be opened in a month. Gisele accepted, pleased with the offer.

The new supermarket, on Visconde de Pirajá, where most of Ipanema's commerce is concentrated, was inaugurated on the appointed date. It was a huge store, much bigger and more sophisticated than the one in Méier, with many aisles full of shelves with thousands of products, many of them imported. At the back of the store there was a butcher, a fish counter, a bakery, and a wine and liquor section. The canned goods section was spacious, and one could find cheeses and delicacies from around the world. Gisele liked her new uniform, the black pants and gray jacket with the logo of the supermarket looked better than what she had worn in the Méier branch. One thing that impressed her was that the customers only paid with credit cards, even for a minimal purchase. Only domestic servants, it was easy to identify them by their clothing, paid in cash. One thing that happened, just as before, was that women asked the price of a product if it was not visible on the merchandise, before they rang it up. Men never asked.

On Saturday a storm hit the city. Traffic was chaotic and Gisele arrived home at eleven at night after a long day of work. Because the street where she lived did not have a sidewalk and was on a hill, a great deal of dirty water and mud had flooded the house.

Maria da Graça woke her daughter before dawn to have her help clean the front and the back of the house. Gisele poured the water with a bucket and the mother scrubbed the floor with a straw broom. Maria da Graça, who had a loud voice, started to sing a carnival tune, the daughter accompanied her and laughed as her mother swayed her hips. They cleaned up the mud little by little, without hurrying, dancing to Maria da Graça's music. Gisele enjoyed her mother's clowning around. Afterward, they had breakfast and then decided to bake a cake to eat when Gisele got back from the beach. She was happy when she saw the sun come out. She got ready with care because she knew she would run into Henrique.

It was ten in the morning when Gisele descended the stairway that connected the top of the hill, where her house was located, to the main street. All the streets in the area were dirt roads, except for the stairway of tile and cement that had been constructed by the people who lived in the neighborhood, with material bought with their own money. Gisele was still a girl when the project had been done, and she and other children helped with the construction. The community was proud of the one hundred thirty-six steps which they had built to create a walkway to the top of the hill.

The sun was very strong when she got to the beach, for it was already past one.

As soon as the volleyball game was over Henrique went to sit down next to Gisele under the umbrella.

The afternoon began to lengthen and once again Henrique asked for Gisele's telephone number, which she did not give him. She looked at him quietly. He embraced her and kissed her on the lips. They sat side by side holding hands, looking at the rough ocean. The sun set behind the mountains and the sky turned an orange rose color.

"I have to go, it's getting late," she said getting up. He did the same.

"Please don't come with me," she said.

She walked in the opposite direction of Henrique's street. When she got to Copacabana, she took the bus.

On Monday, as usual, Gisele woke up in the dark to go to work.

The cash register where she was stationed was at the right-hand corner of the supermarket entrance. Around eleven, Gisele saw Henrique looking for something on the shelves. It was him, she was certain. She got nervous, could he have seen her?

As soon as she finished waiting on a customer, she put up a sign that the register was closed and she went out to talk with the manager. She said she was feeling ill and that she needed to rest for a while. The manager suggested she go to the ladies' room to rest.

In the ladies' room she felt calmer. Even so, her heart was beating fast—had he seen her? It was all she could think about. An hour later she called the manager and said that she was not feeling better and would like to go home. The manager told her to take care of herself and to return when she felt better.

When her mother returned from work she was surprised to see Gisele at home so early, normally she did not get home until after nine and it was only seven o'clock.

"Mother, I was laid off. They are reducing the number of workers. I am going to lie down for a while, I'm not feeling well. But don't worry. It was for the best. Ipanema is a long way from home."

Happiness is wanting something you can have.

Translated by Elizabeth Lowe

A Thing of Beauty

Fred Góes

IT'S NOT THAT THE APARTMENT is badly located. Not at all. It's in an upscale area of the city. For some time now it's come in the line of fire. But not as much as the media say. It's not like you can't survive. You can. The thing is to stay alert. I'm not about to let down my guard.

So what if there's a curfew? We just go to sleep earlier, okay? There's nothing in life that with a bit of good will we can't adjust to.

It's all a question of code, of semiotics, as the French teacher who lives in the building says. When the spec-

FRED GÓES was born in 1948 in Rio de Janeiro, and is a professor in the Faculty of Letters at the Universidade Federal there, his specialty being Carnival Studies. Composer, lyricist, short story writer, and essayist, he edited an anthology of Carnival stories and essays *Brasil, Mostra a sua Máscara (Brazil, Show Your Mask.)* This story, a finalist in a fiction contest sponsored by Rio's leading newspaper, appeared in the anthology *Contos do Rio (Stories of Rio).* In its brevity and wit, it is a virtually flawless vignette that epitomizes the characteristic long-suffering good humor of the *carioca* (natives of Rio). By making a joke of some of the more harrowing tribulations of urban life, he creates a buffer that helps the reader cope with the anxieties that beset inhabitants of that metropolis of over eight million.

tacle of *son et lumière* begins, after the first signal flare and the growl of the first burst of gunfire, you just crawl. Cover the windows using a practiced technique, turn out all the lights. Die a little. From fright.

Since it's all but impossible to eat lying on your stomach, we've opted to have dinner in the elevator, which opens to all four apartments on the floor. It's unbelievable, but the conviviality and solidarity among neighbors has grown much stronger lately. Here on the tenth, for example, we usually watch, all of us together, the nine o'clock soap on Dona Branca's TV. Her living room is in a privileged location, protected from stray bullets. The same can't be said of the bedrooms.

My wife is already so accustomed to the situation that she's even ordered slipcovers for the barricades in the living room, which replace the furniture these days, in a more subtle camouflage pattern. As a Christmas present for the family, besides the shatterproof windows, I've ordered bulletproof vests, a bit lighter now that it's summer. The only thing that's a nuisance is the helmets we're forced to wear even when asleep. They heat up your head a little. But it's not all that unbearable.

On the balcony next to the living room, I put in two parallel concrete walls and replaced the glass with steel. But I made a point of leaving a hole through which, on calmer days, we could stick our heads.

You have to see it. What a thing of beauty! Gávea Rock, Two Brothers mountain, Bonita Rock, Sumaré, and the statue of Christ the Redeemer on top of Corcovado.

Translated by Clifford Landers

The Virtuous Wife

Julieta de Godoy Ladeira

Hydrangea Fest in Granada. Coffee Fest in Ribeirão Preto. Strawberries in Suzano, the sea in Rio Grande. Soy Fest in Itararé.

THE TYPEWRITTEN PAGE—"we have transcribed below, for your information, the commemorative dates for the month of December"—was all they found (according

JULIETA DE GODOY LADEIRA (1935–1997) authored several volumes of short stories, a novel, and children's literature. She received one of Brazil's most distinguished literary prizes, the Jabuti, for her collection of stories, *Passe as ferias em Nassau.* She also collaborated on writing projects with her husband Osman Lins, author of acclaimed novel *Avolovara.* Her works have been translated into German, Spanish, Polish, and English. This story is from her 1978 collection *Dia de matar o patrão* (*Day to Kill the Boss*), in which she focuses her attention on the Brazilian upper middle class, especially those in business, whose world she knew firsthand from working in advertising. She depicts lonely people searching for a meaning that remains just beyond their grasp.

to his colleagues) on the desk in his office, next to the company telephone and slide rule.

He died on a weekend. He left two sons, one twenty, the other eighteen. The death throes must have lasted for a few minutes, not many, according to the doctors who examined him afterwards. His former lover is standing in the crowd around the coffin. Desolate, weeping softly, now and then she leaves to sob discreetly in some corner or hallway. She gave me a slight nod while barely noticing me. She was completely absorbed in the deceased (he was my husband). She leaned over his face and studied it in silence and with rapt attention. She wanted to touch it, her hand stopped halfway, she stepped back with a moan (I think I was the only one who heard).

Department of the Navy Week. Tea Fest in Registro.
Opening of the beach season.

We were in Guarujá expecting him to arrive on Saturday night or Sunday morning.

"Are you going to make me do this after working all week? Solid gridlock all the way down the mountain. Why the hell do I have to show my face here?"

Well, I spent every day sunbathing, napping in the afternoon, playing cards, so it was natural to want to dine out or go to a nightclub on Saturday. Any crime in that?

The boys hang out on the beach until all hours, it's no use calling them, they don't obey anymore. This year they wanted to go up the coast to Ubatuba with their friends but I wouldn't let them, they're better off with me, they'll keep out of trouble. I got in around two, I took off my sandals in the kitchen, I didn't want to drag sand into the other rooms. The table, set for lunch. Smell of fish, heat from the oven, maid sweating. The rest of the apartment pleasant, windows open, curtains billowing. Bedrooms already straightened up, afternoon light filtering through closed blinds and casting crisp geometric shapes on walls, across beds and closets. Large rooms, two and a half baths. At first I was against the place. I wanted to avoid the headache of double duty.

My mother was of the same opinion: "You're going to be stuck there every Saturday and Sunday. That's just what he wants. You're better off staying in different hotels, seaside resorts, meeting interesting people. And if you don't have a maid . . . "

I realized later he'd made the right choice: reasonable price and increasing value. But I never let on I felt that way.

After lunch, still drying my hair on the terrace, I looked for the boys so I could signal for them to come up. The telephone rang, I received the news: "Your husband has taken sick." He was already dead.

The fifth, founding of the Red Cross. The sixth, the battle of Itororó is joined (1868), during the Paraguayan War.

Another boy. Our second and last child. An accident. We didn't want him. It was dismaying to watch my youth pass by in obscurity. I wanted to travel—Mediterranean cruises, embassy dinners, romance in Antibes. A preposterous lifestyle for that cautious, withdrawn, unenthusiastic man. He convinced himself that increasing his earnings would make our life together more bearable. Or did

I convince him? He took on a second job and we hardly ever saw each other.

He complained, "You forgot to buy soap again. We're out of toilet paper. This salad dressing doesn't taste right."

Seamstress, stores, mother's house, beauty parlor. They asked me if I could feel the baby kick yet, they taught me stitches for quilts and shawls, they talked about childbirth and childhood illness. He'd arrive late, and I'd leave a plate covered with a napkin and go to bed. I'd ask him not to light the stove so the burners wouldn't get dirty and not to leave matchsticks in the sink. The food got cold but he could always go to a restaurant, there were several near his office. I did what I could. After all, I was half asleep by the time he showed up. I didn't know what to talk about: the boys, the maid? It was too late for that. His job? The hours he spent away from home fell like a shadow between us, an empty space, an abyss I never approached. At least my pregnancy relieved the monotony. Afterward we separated.

The seventh: the Japanese attack the American naval base at Pearl Harbor.

He moved into a hotel. My mother advised me not to chase after him, "He'll come back."

Loneliness came in frightening forms—decide, explain, start over, list the reasons, find my own center, the grounds, the means to go on—but I had been the weak link in my own life and so I lost whatever balance I'd kept up till then. I dressed the oldest boy, took him to the office, made him repeat over and over what he should say to his father, and put him in the elevator with instructions to the operator.

I walked through the city feeling as if I were floating past people, objects, lighted shop windows, my body unfurling banners in the hope of a joyless victory representing my quest for peace of mind.

They arrived at dinnertime. The boy, half asleep; his father, cloaked in a morose silence he would rarely ever break again. Later, during our endless squabbles, he said in many different tones that he'd never understand why I used a child to force him to come back.

The eighth: Justice Day, Sportswriters Day, Police Officers Day, Family Day, Day of Our Lady of Conception.

He died at home, naked, squatting in the shower stall. A bullet in his head. It was the peak of the summer season and we had to take down our clothes, still wet on the line, and rush back. Amidst the whir of the fan and the smell of the flowers that partially cover his body, the headache and the weariness that paralyze me, I wonder why he didn't wait, he would've had the whole winter to do it, and I remember the fragrance of the lotion he always used and the stench of cigarettes that permeated his skin, his clothes, any place he found himself. And these different odors, these faces that approach, bow down slightly, move away, and the hair of that woman, the only one really crying for him, all remind me of the broad marble entryway to the apartment where we spent the last years, his vases of ferns and anthuriums, wrought-iron benches, the timeless atmosphere of a spa or a cemetery, where his footsteps echoed without producing vibration, the hesitant way he walked through the living room, dodging the Portuguese Renaissance furniture, the alabaster pendants, on the way to his bedroom, which he hadn't shared with me since his return home.

Beginning of the Bonfim and Conceição Beach Festivals (Bahia).

Following his doctor's advice, he went on a trip to recover from exhaustion brought on by overwork. For the first time, I went to meet his company's directors, this was my chance to request a small advance, I claimed he hadn't left me enough to meet expenses. Maybe that way they'd see I was on to the scheme they and the doctor had doubtless cooked up for those odd vacation trips far from his family. They brought up the strain of his last year, the risk of a heart attack (it was news to me). I didn't say much, cautiously avoiding traps, not wanting them to realize how poorly informed I was. I didn't know them, I had never accepted their invitations, I thought that his "friends from the office" must be vulgar, their wives without class, they were part of his life and his business affairs, not mine. They proved to be courteous, coffee was served, and when I made my exit, check in hand, one of them saw me to the elevator. "He needs support, a little understanding." The door opened, I entered, and when I started down I left behind a face with an apologetic, forced smile.

The tenth: Declaration of the Rights of Man.

I left the car in the parking lot and to avoid showing up early for our appointment I walked for a while through the narrow *gallerias*. Boutiques offering perfume, lighters, Japanese pencil cases, dolls in transparent boxes, trinkets, cafés suffused with daylight, musty smells, something mysterious of unknown origin. Five o'clock, Excelsior Hotel Bar. He was finishing a sweet vermouth when I arrived. He stood up and when he pulled out a chair his hands were shaking. How long had it been, how many years since we'd met alone in a public place? I wasn't certain why it was so urgent he talk to me, but I had an idea. I ordered a crème de menthe, arranged my purse, and waited. After a few of the usual questions—"The traffic bad? The boys eat a proper lunch?"—he got to the point. Today at least you've got to hear me out. To understand and go along. In other words, an amicable separation. I would keep the house, the car, the children. The alimony would be reasonable. His voice was unsteady, he spoke softly, but some sort of unexpected emotion seemed to take hold of his words and then shake them and spew them out. The bluish cast of the buildings began to darken, the neon signs blinked on, the waiter replaced the ashtray and put another dish of cashews and peanuts on the table, and I traveled mentally through the shopping malls, all, several, hundreds of malls that seemed to go on endlessly, I guided my long lost youth through exotic cities, I bathed in sacred rivers, I saw myself naked in icy waters, my sex like snow, edelweiss sprouting from my breasts and belly.

"I don't think it's the right thing for the boys."

"They're men now!"

"I have to look after them. I've always been a good mother, you know that."

"It would be better if they lived with the truth."

The cook has probably left already, today's the day to scrub the terrace, clean the leaves of the plants, polish the silver. He can't complain, everything is bright and shiny, the boys are healthy, I make sure they dress warmly when they go out, wash behind the ears, don't leave the bathroom wet after their showers; I keep a close check on the pantry, I have the filter cleaned, I always look at receipts to make sure I don't get shortchanged, I insist on cleanliness and orderliness at home, I take communion the first Friday of every month.

"There must be another woman."

"And what if there is? Did you ever care about what I am, do, think?"

The maids don't dillydally, I make sure they're out of bed early, the boys don't have any friends, they spend Sundays with me, I protect them from bad influences. I walk discreetly when I'm out, men never turn around to look at me.

"No, I won't agree to a separation. It goes against my upbringing."

He was so sure it would be easy to bend me to his will. His mistake. He'd have to report back to a woman who was doubtless glancing anxiously at her watch, at the telephone. There was something intriguing about deciding the fate of a person I'd never met.

The eleventh: Kennel Club Dog Show, Água Branca Park (São Paulo)

A married woman. A matron. Birthday teas, holidays in Guarujá, thyroid medication.

Isn't that what I was prepared for all through my childhood and adolescence, my family's obsession, the single and constant expectation? Marriage: quest, absolution, salvation. Forests of clinging vines watered daily by mothers, grandmothers, doctors, teachers, seamstresses, sisters of charity, manicures, vitamins, to grow on tree trunks and suck out their sap, their strength, or on walls whose clay, deprived of sunlight, will one day rot and crumble on the grass in the yard or the tiles in the bathroom. He was the first man to ask me to marry him. We lived on the same block. He was young, he wanted an uncomplicated woman who didn't wear makeup, had few friends and limited horizons.

It's a role easily played, requiring minimal talent. Why wait? No career, little beauty. Wide hips, prominent belly. Baby maker. Lacking the courage to face the simplest choices or challenges.

My trousseau included linen sheets, handmade lingerie, imported lace, vicuña quilts, monogrammed blankets and bath and dishtowels. I relaxed my muscles in that soothing refuge, comfortably lined my spirit with velvet, and never signed a check because it was easier for him to withdraw cash from the bank downtown, never made household purchases because he said my math was lousy and it was no trouble for him to do the marketing; not even the baby bottles were my concern, I might get the formula wrong—he filled them before going out. His advice on temperature: "test it on the back of your hand." He phoned regularly to check if everything was OK. I was the woman in the bell jar, who knows nothing, who is afraid, a glass bird, "my wife is inexperienced," rituals protected me, I knew how to follow them, through habit they soaked into my skin, I fell into a stupor I couldn't wake up from, aware that so much as opening my eyes or reaching out my arms would be difficult, painful acts, immobility and estrangement were preferable. "She can't live alone. She's defenseless."

The thirteenth: Bible Day.

Winters and summers passed, mornings on the beach, holidays in the country, commencement exercises, acquaintances' deaths, different maids, family get-togethers, Sundays that dragged on, Saturdays when he went out in a sport shirt and came back with the scent of a woman and vermouth, ate a big lunch, and went to sleep. Later on he went out to buy cigarettes or a newspaper—he made phone calls. More than once I followed him out of curiosity. Short calls from the bakery or the drugstore, perhaps only to say goodnight. He would walk back slowly, calm now. For a long time this romance went on between working hours and his obligatory and burdensome presence at home, however brief. Saturday mornings created the longest pause, the illusion of permanence. He went out before eight, his face cut by a hasty shave, the bottle of lotion sometimes left open by the sink. They met in an apartment on Marechal Deodoro Plaza, later in another on Santo Antonio Street, which I visited one afternoon when I knew they'd be at work. I saw the address on a rent receipt I found in his billfold. I made a mold of all his keys, had them copied, tried them, and one worked. I slowly pushed open the door and saw a narrow hallway appear. I fearfully tiptoed in like a burglar. Built-in refrigerator over the sink. Just a room with a bar, sofa bed, closet, easy chairs, large mirror, gray carpet, and faded curtains. I sat on the armrest of one of

the chairs. I kept away from the sofa. No pictures, not a
single item of clothing beyond the bath towels. I opened
the closet. Sheets and a blanket folded on top of two pil-
lows. In one corner, an unopened bottle of liqueur inside
its Christmas wrappings. I found letters in one of the
drawers. Gift paper and ribbons neatly stored in a wooden
box. An envelope with small greeting cards. Tall, narrow
handwriting, the kind learned in convent schools. Letters, reflecting various moods, which I nervously scanned.
Some talked about a possible life together, perhaps in the
near future, marriage, children, plans. Others written
during nights of insomnia, crisis, panic over the life they
led, no solution, postcards from several cities where he'd
gone on business. An almost childish form of expression
that was new and strange to me in the handwriting I had
seen so often on checks, receipts, and notes he occasionally had to leave at home.

I left feeling some of the cold in that room where the
sunlight probably never penetrated, feeling the sadness,
sometimes sweet, other times brittle and resentful, which
permeated their life together. Two souls so close and yet
so lost on a path I had blocked. A sense that their hours
passed by too quickly to use up words and gestures. No
erotic sensation, merely the impression of a modest apartment belonging to two white-collar workers just starting
out. By the sink, two cheap, clean glasses turned upside
down on a checkered cloth. A tin of crackers, paper
napkins.

Two years later she attempted suicide. I remember
how devastated he was when he showed up well after
dinner, his irritation, pacing the bedroom floor all night,

prolonged absences, driving off in the early morning. He brought up the subject again. He pleaded. I refused to budge. There was no brave new world out there for me.

"No. Separation goes against my upbringing."

"Then I'll just up and leave."

"You won't have anything to start over with. I have proof of your adultery."

I showed him the key and he recognized it. He was stunned. The young woman underwent lengthy treatment, she spent several months resting in a sanitorium, she moved to Rio. They both got old so fast.

Twenty first: beginning of summer.

When the driver opened the door for me one rainy morning, and I slipped on the curb and twisted my ankle, a man appeared out of nowhere to help me. As I touched his hand I felt a long-forgotten warmth pass from his fingers to mine. I tested my ankle; it hurt but I pulled away as soon as I could to avoid prying eyes. Why, at nearly the same time, had I told the driver not to wait for me, to return home with the car, when I'd just gone out to do a little shopping in that store?

His name was Nogueira, from the Intermundial Bank. For three and a half years we met in the hotel where he'd been staying since his transfer from Brasília. He wanted to get married abroad. There were times I almost gave in. But I wasn't up to facing a new situation, I was satisfied with the one I had, and this way my husband would have no chance to live with that woman. Nogueira gave up. I'm not sure why—my heart grown cold or my endless misgivings. Fine. I was sick of going to the hairdresser every Thursday and meeting him afterward at four thirty.

Christmas. Lifeguard Day. São Silvestre Run.

I can visualize clearly the hat I'll wear to the requiem mass. Light makeup, small veil covering my eyes. I'll need to alter the hemline of my black suit, it's out of fashion. Two of his relatives support me, holding my arms as the boys shed their tears across the way, a pitiful, moaning cry. They don't look at me. Dark sky, wind, they've lowered the coffin, the silence broken only by the sound of wet concrete shoveled on top of the lid. Mr. Guimarães, our attorney, told me to call him without delay, he's ready to do the inventory. My sisters-in-law and women friends show their concern:

"He meant everything to her. What'll she do without him?"

"Such a senseless act. Poor thing, she doesn't have a clue why he did it."

His friends from the office said he'd worked late the night before and he'd bought a newspaper on the way to the parking lot. His parting words: "See you on Monday, have a nice weekend, I'd stay here and rest up if I could, but you know how it is, my family's on holiday."

Could he have made a sudden decision later on? Utterly ridiculous. My sisters-in-law and Guimarães will try to tell me what to do. They've got another thing coming. I don't want to have to deal with paperwork, notaries, I'll accept their—the family's and the lawyer's—help in that area, but as to the property, we'll see, maybe it'll be my lucky day. And then Europe, sell the house, buy a condo in the Higiénpolis district or on a cross street of Avenida Paulista. They've finally closed the grave. Everyone is considerate, they take me to the car, to all the waiting cars, in each and every one a place for me, and they want to keep me company, make some soup, tea, all my female friends and relatives are prepared to spend the night with me, comfort me, it's like being carried on a litter. At the corner of Avenida Dr. Arnaldo we pass by the blond woman signaling for a taxi, it doesn't stop, she's partly bent over as she continues up the sidewalk alone, on her way to where?

Translation by David George

Architect by Correspondence

by Marcos Rey

MY HOUSE (I'm speaking of a long time ago) served for many years as a place of hospitality for nearly unknown relatives who came from the interior for a visit or to try their luck in the capital. Some stayed at our house because they couldn't find a vacancy in a hotel, some because they didn't like hotels, and others because they preferred family living. Cousin Emílio was one of these. In the letter advising us of his arrival he made it clear that he had the means

---

Under the pseudonym MARCOS REY, São Paulo-born Edmundo Donato (1925–1999) gained national recognition with *Memórias de um Gigolô*, published in English in 1987 as *Memoirs of a Gigolo*. A modern picaresque novel, it became an all-time best seller and later a popular television miniseries. A winner of the coveted Jabuti prize, Rey published novels and short stories regularly, beginning as a teenager. Often chronicling the nocturnal world of hustlers and loose women, he let readers form their own conclusions, never imposing his own view of his fictional creations. This story, which depicts a less complicated time seen through innocent eyes, is required reading in Brazilian middle schools.

---

to rent a beautiful downtown apartment or a comfortable house in a quiet neighborhood but feared offending our spirit of hospitality. "I'm dying to see you," the letter ended.

The mailman never brought my family a more surprising letter. Emílio was a distant cousin, out of circulation and completely forgotten. I knew him only through a yellowing photo in the family album. Emílio, with a straw hat on his head and a bow tie, standing in front of a monkey cage at the zoo. A lovely picture!

The letter came at eleven; at noon Emílio rang our doorbell with his suitcase and his charm. Of course he no longer wore a straw hat, but the black bow tie was there, decorating his slim neck.

"Hi, folks! Here I am, Emílio!"

Cousin Emílio was a man of medium height with a cylindrical body and a small, oval face. He was young in spirit, but his hair was graying at the temples. He had to dye it monthly, as I learned later. He smoked like a man possessed, Petit Londrino brand, and often spat, without looking. When he was satisfied with something he would rub his hands, a habit we often laughed at. And he liked to say "Fine and dandy!" even when things weren't fine.

The day he arrived he spoke of only one thing throughout lunch: his aversion to hotels and the hordes of insects that plagued his nights of loneliness and insomnia. Mom was so moved that she almost cried when Cousin Emílio confessed:

"I was once an ingrate, aunt. To heck with relatives, I said. It's true; I was like that. But suffering taught me to value relatives and to pray that they never lack for health and money."

Not only my mother; everybody was moved.

"Did you come all this way with anything in mind?" my father asked.

"I'm going to put up buildings. Did you know that São Paulo is the fastest growing city in the world?"

"You're a contractor?"

"Me, a contractor? I'm an architect!"

"What about your degree?"

"I'll get it in December, if I pass my exams."

"What college are you at, Emílio?"

"A college in Rio de Janeiro."

"How's that possible if you don't live there?"

He paused and confided: "I'm going to get my degree by correspondence." Amid the general disbelief he added: "Nowadays only the incompetent actually attend school. This is the Twentieth Century, isn't it? Everything these days is highly practical. That's why they invented these courses. A friend of mine is even studying surgery by correspondence . . ."

My father said thoughtfully, "Would you trust your insides to a surgeon who'd gotten a correspondence degree?"

"Of course I would. I think . . ."

To give him his due, Cousin Emílio was no idler. He would rise early, drink his coffee and cream, and quickly head for the street. Sometimes he would return within half an hour. He was the first at the table for dinner. Immediately afterward he would leave with the same haste, and the poor man would stay out until early morning. We imagined that, even before getting his degree, he had already begun construction work, since he was a man who hated to waste time.

One day Emílio announced at lunch, "I start tomorrow."

"Where's the first building going to be?" Mom asked.

"Building? What do you mean, Aunt?"

"Aren't you going to construct buildings?"

Cousin Emílio began to laugh heartily, shaking his head.

"There are too many construction firms as it is."

"Then what *are* you going to do?" my father asked.

Cousin Emílio went to his room, the one in the rear from which we'd had to displace the maid, and returned triumphantly with several packages, which he placed on the table. It was as if he had brought gold dust, for the packages contained powder, as he quickly showed us.

"This is one fine deal."

"What kind of deal?"

"I'm going to manufacture liquor."

"Liquor?"

"That yellow powder is Scotch whiskey. This one is a delightful vermouth. This other one is Rio Grande wine. Fine drinks like those they used to make before the war. It's the greatest business in the world!"

"What about a distillery? Won't you need one?"

"A trifle!"

It wasn't until the next morning, a Saturday, that we learned the details of Cousin Emílio's industrial plans. He was right; there was no need for a distillery. All he needed was powder, alcohol, and water. And one other thing: our old bathtub, retired years before to a corner of the back yard. Rubbing his hands with great optimism, and appointing me his assistant, he went to work. As soon as the liquid was the right color he took a wooden spoon, plunged it into the tub, and raised it to his mouth. He withdrew it quickly.

"More powder!" he exclaimed.

I handed him another package, which he immediately dumped into the tub.

The liquid, which was blue, changed to a greenish color, then began to turn yellow, and finally purple.

"A lovely color!" my cousin said in admiration.

The second step was to fill the bottles. Cousin Emílio had bought several dozen empty bottles. I eagerly helped him with his task. But his day wasn't over yet. There were still the labels. He had a wad of them—colorful, attractive, written in English. Didactically, Emílio taught me the meaning of some of the words, like *made, finest, Scotland,* and many others. His pronunciation probably wasn't all that good, but he was very happy.

For two months I helped Cousin Emílio manufacture the liquor and fill the bottles, as well as glue on the labels. At times such an uncertain color resulted that no one in the house could make it out; so Emílio would stick on a label reading "Antillean Rum." It was a drink in great demand, as I was later to confirm.

Cousin Emílio did well as an industrialist, at least at first. The bathtub was always full and he bought hundreds of empty bottles. I remember, to the incredible amazement of all, that he even paid my father rent on the back room. On Sundays he would bring a large bottle of wine to the table, not of his manufacture but purchased in a neighborhood store. He expanded his wardrobe and began going out every night, perfumed and acting like a dandy.

One day Cousin Emílio said, "I'm going to move. I'm

thinking of buying a house. But I'll take the tub with me. I'll pay fifty dollars for it."

"For that price you can buy several new bathtubs," my father said.

"I know, but I'm very grateful to that tub. I said fifty. I'll pay right now."

"Right now?"

"I mean, tomorrow."

The next morning two men in hats appeared at the door. Cousin Emílio went to greet them with open arms. But they weren't buyers. They displayed badges behind their lapels and carried off the industrialist, along with a pack of "Antillean Rum" labels.

Cousin Emílio spent three days explaining things at the police station. It turned out that, like everyone, the police detective took a liking to him and set him free on the condition that he promise never again to manufacture domestic or foreign spirits. Cousin Emílio returned home, but not crushed as we had supposed. He was an optimistic man and full of ideas.

"I'll work something out," he promised at the table, adjusting his tie. "In this world only those who never try are defeated."

He went at once to the backyard and stood looking at the bathtub for a long time.

"I'm going to sell it for scrap," my father said.

"I said I'd buy the tub and I don't go back on my word."

"To manufacture liquor? Anything but that!"

"I have another idea," he said mysteriously, before retiring to his room to meditate.

The next day, Cousin Emílio left early to buy a bellows. That's right, a bellows. When asked what it was, he didn't reply. He was clearly in high gear. My father discovered that he had commissioned a large sign, nine feet high by six feet wide. He dragged the bathtub to his room, after making a few repairs in it. He went around checking the plumbing in the house, and, without asking permission, had part of his modest room tiled, at the same time that he had dark, thick glass installed in the window. Finally, he found a print shop in the neighborhood and ordered thousands of flyers.

Everyone in the family was concerned about all that commotion, but there was no need to drag it out of him.

"Now I can speak frankly, partner," he told my father.

"What are you getting at?"

"Pay close attention, partner."

"First explain why you're calling me partner."

"Gladly."

As he was explaining, the doorbell rang. It was deliverymen with the aforementioned 9' x 6' sign. We all went to the door with curiosity, but knowing that he would explain everything. In astonishment my father read: "THE SULTAN OF TURKISH BATHS—*Rheumatism, arthritis, problems of the spine, paralysis in general—Hot and cold showers, using the up-to-the-minute Emilius Method.*"

"You can hang the sign in front," Emílio told the deliverymen. Turning to my father, he said, "Do you mind tipping them, partner?"

Back at the table, happy and fulfilled but not without appetite, Emílio spoke of the miracles that Turkish baths had achieved in curing circulatory ills. The extremes of hot and cold had raised longtime paralytics from their sickbeds. He had read all about it and harbored no doubts.

As for the Emilius Method, he acknowledged it was just a gimmick, something different: cold air applied to the spine with a bellows. But if it did no good, it also did no harm.

"And you intend to see your customers in that tiny back room?" my mother asked.

"Sick people are looking for a cure, not comfort."

"Have you tried it out?"

"Not personally, but the Turks did it long before me. They have centuries of experience. Did any of you ever see a rheumatic Turk? Well, did you?"

"I can't remember," my father admitted.

"There you are. If you had, you wouldn't have forgotten."

My father still resisted the partnership despite the fortune to be made with the bathhouse.

"What about the license, Emílio? Do you have a license to run a business?"

Cousin Emílio got up in the middle of dessert, remembering that he had to go by the print shop to pick up the adverts, as he called them, to distribute around the neighborhood. Emílio was always a great believer in publicity and was the first person I ever heard say, "Advertising is the soul of business."

As soon as Cousin Emílio left, I went to the door to take a better look at the sign, which was causing consternation among the neighbors, mostly because lack of water was the major problem on our street. He returned in the early evening after distributing most of the pamphlets. He must have felt very enthusiastic about it all, for I'd never seen him smoke a cigar before, which he was now doing with great satisfaction.

The next morning, unlike his usual custom, Emílio rose early and began walking around the house, perhaps in expectation of his first client. He waited in vain the entire day, pacing impatiently. Two days later he decided to go out, remembering that the owner of the grocery store suffered from a painful limp in one leg. He tried to sell him on a twelve-bath treatment. Although each bath was extremely cheap, the man preferred to keep his paraplegic leg. We found out that Emílio had an ugly fight with him and didn't punch him, by way of persuasion, only because he owed a small sum at the store.

There were no customers the first week. The second week there was one, but he changed his mind when he saw the enormous bellows that produced the gush of air on the spine. At the end of a month we were all sure Emílio's undertaking had failed. He was already seeing about getting the sign removed when a car pulled up and his great hope got out.

Got out? No, *was gotten* out. What I saw was a little old man carried on the arms of two husky grandsons. They placed him in an armchair. He was holding one of Emílio's pamphlets in his trembling hand.

"Please, I'd like to see Dr. Emílio."

My mother, frightened at the sick man's condition and hoping to avoid complications, was explaining that Dr. Emílio was away, when he burst into the parlor wearing a smile that would have inspired confidence and assurance of cure in any paraplegic in the world.

"Here I am!" he exclaimed, as if to say: here's salvation. "What's your problem? Ah yes, the legs! Lower your pants so I can take a look at them."

The examination was brief.

"What do you think, doctor?"

"It's a cinch!"

"A cinch?"

"A cinch."

Emílio immediately led him by the arm to the back room, his customer wailing and grumbling the entire time. Waiting in the parlor were his grandsons and my mother and father, who were secretly praying. I went to the backyard, near the room at the rear, since at the age of twelve I was the only member of the family who believed in the miracles that Emílio could achieve through baths, steam and bellows.

At the beginning the old man seemed to hold out well against the ordeal. Perhaps the hot water soothed him. But things got worse when that enormous piece of ice arrived from the grocer's. Then the aged customer began moaning louder and louder. One of the grandsons knocked at the door in fright, but Emílio answered that this was how it was done and that everything was all right. Still, the groans turned to screams with the application of the blast of cold air to the spine. I thought the old man was done for, had kicked the bucket, bitten the dust. And apparently everyone, including the entire neighborhood, had the same impression.

When the ambulance arrived, Emílio's customer was no longer moaning; he was stiff and frozen. My cousin, still at the bellows, promised the grandsons that the old man would exhibit greater resistance at the second bath. And he mentioned numerous paraplegics who, he said, frequented his clinic with fine results. But they weren't listening, and, in addition to not paying for the bath, insulted Cousin Emílio.

"That's what comes from dealing with ignorant people," lamented the sultan of Turkish baths. "But if you expect to come back, don't count on me!"

I never saw anyone sadder than Cousin Emílio the day they took the sign down from the front of the house. His world was crumbling, his last hope had run aground. Disillusioned, he packed his bags to return to the interior, but he didn't go. He stayed, trying to come up with new ideas, racking his brains all day long. My mother tired of his company and asked him for his bed because the maid didn't want to sleep on the sofa any longer.

He gave back the bed, saying, "It doesn't matter. I'll sleep in the bathtub."

He must have liked the tub, since he never left it before noon.

I remember it was Christmas Eve, my cousin quite discredited in the family, when the mail brought a cardboard tube wrapped in tissue paper. I took it from the mailman and went to his room. My cousin was snoring in the bathtub, wearing what had once been pajamas. Since he had run out of money to dye his hair, he had grayed considerably. I noticed that his old straw hat was being used as an ashtray. And his inseparable tie no longer had any color, like "Antillean Rum."

I woke my cousin with some difficulty and handed him the tube. Emílio, still drowsy, preferred to sleep a while longer rather than open it. We were about to sit down for lunch when he burst impetuously into the parlor smiling hysterically and brandishing the tube in the air.

"My diploma! I passed the exams! I have a degree! You hear? I have a degree!"

It was a beautiful and solemn diploma, neatly printed in gothic letters, sealed, stamped, and covered with signatures on both sides.

"See, everything is in order," my cousin said. "And legal, just the way I've always insisted on things."

My father, who had never taken my cousin seriously, was forced to admit his mistake.

"That Emílio is really something! A college degree by correspondence! Who would have thought it?"

"And I graduated with a good average—95."

"Ninety-five is a grade and then some, man!"

Emílio's happiness made that Christmas unforgettable. He ran to the market and ordered a turkey with money that my father lent him, which in no way diminished the value of the gesture. In addition, he bought some Christmas decorations on our account and set up a beautiful tree in the corner of the parlor. Not even Santa Claus was as busy as Emílio for the next few days. As for the diploma, he ordered a heavy gilded frame made for it and hung it in the hallway for all to see as they passed by. The same print shop that did the publicity flyers for the "sultan of the Turkish baths" ran off a thousand visiting cards: "Emílio So-and-So, B.A., Architect."

He spent the rest of that year designing at a drawing board that Mom gave him. He felt himself with sufficient energy to revolutionize architecture and earn mountains of money. He explained some of his designs in detail, among them an immense hospital for the middle class, which he saw as a neglected group. At midnight at the New Year's Eve party, as children in the street banged on lampposts and sirens sounded, he made an intimate and emotional announcement: Cousin Emílio was going to get married.

"You don't know about it, but for twenty years I've been engaged to a nice girl back home. I guess she must be getting tired of waiting, but now that some money will be coming in, I'll marry her. It's time to start acting sensibly!"

This revelation brought tears to the family's eyes and inspired my father to rush out and buy a few more bottles of wine as the moment demanded.

In the first days of January, with Cousin Emílio already wearing a class ring on his finger, it happened: an item in the paper, on the last page, dedicated to the police blotter. The news referred to a veritable diploma mill for college degrees, located in Rio de Janeiro, whose president was already behind bars. There followed a list of "graduates" who had been taken in, including the name of Cousin Emílio.

My cousin was the last one in the house to read the news. No one had the courage to show him the newspaper. But it had to be done, before he got hired as an architect by some construction firm and ended up in jail too. Emílio laid his eyes on the page, understood, and collapsed into a chair. For some time he was silent and deaf to the family's words of consolation. Afterwards, he rose and went to the room in the rear.

"Is he going to kill himself?" my mother said fearfully.

In fact that was what all of us were afraid of. But he didn't kill himself. In his room he found a little of the colored powder and a bottle of alcohol and in a short time manufactured the amount of liquor needed for the desired effect. When he returned to the parlor, where everyone was waiting for him, his legs were wobbly and his head seemed to be spinning. We tried to get him to sit down, but he preferred to circle about the table. On one of his turns he lost his balance and fell. He seemed on the point of vomiting, sitting there on the sofa. We spread a newspaper on the floor. When he saw the newspaper he lost the urge to vomit. He asked for coffee. The coffee came, but he didn't drink it. He kicked the drawing board.

"Goodbye. I'm going away," he said.

"You can't walk in the streets like that," someone said.

"There's nothing more to keep me here. I'm going back to the interior and marry Joaninha."

Joaninha? That was the first time we'd heard the patient fiancé's name.

"Don't go," my father said.

"I'm leaving," he replied, decisively and reeking of the unmistakable "Antillean Rum."

"At least stay till tomorrow."

"Till tomorrow?"

"You can leave tomorrow."

Emílio concentrated on resolving his indecision. After a long silence, he made up his mind.

"Since you insist, I'll stay today and leave tomorrow."

Cousin Emílio was a man of his word: he stayed. He just forgot the second part of his promise. He didn't leave the next day because it was raining heavily. But five years later he packed his bags and said goodbye. We found out afterward that Joaninha was already married when he got back to the interior. The ingrate. That's the world for you.

Translated by Clifford Landers

The Piece

Álvaro Cardoso Gomes

I'D GONE OUT FOR A SNACK with Bellochio, to a coffee shop on a street just off the Interlagos expressway. It was eleven o'clock at night. We'd just gone inside when we saw three guys holding up the cashier at the register.

"Freeze! Police!" My partner yelled, grabbing his pistol.

The robbers started shooting in no time. We quickly

ÁLVARO CARDOSO GOMES, born in 1944 in Batatais, São Paulo, received his Ph.D. and taught at the Universidade de São Paulo until retirement, specializing in late nineteenth century European poetry and the contemporary novel in Portugal. He has been visiting professor at the University of California Berkeley and visiting writer at Middlebury College. In addition to his prolific production in literary criticism, he has published numerous novels and short stories, including *A teia de aranha*, *O senhor dos porcos*, *Objeto não identificado*, *O sonho da terra*, *Os rios inumeráveis*, *A divina paródia*, *Contracanto*, and *Concerto amazônico*. This short story belongs to the author's realist/ detective series, with *A boneca platinada* and *O comando negro*. The hero, lifted from these two novels, lives in a dehumanizing megalopolis where he often confronts extreme violence.

hunkered down behind the counter. The .45 made a blast in the wall; it was clear they weren't fooling around. We shot back and they took off. We ran after the hoodlums, but they got into an Audi parked in front of the coffee shop. When they hit the gas, in a clumsy move they ran straight into a telephone pole. Bellochio and I started shooting at almost exactly the same time, puncturing the car and shattering one of the side windows. The driver maneuvered rapidly, pulling away from the telephone pole and taking off like wild fire. We got into Bellochio's squad car and started the chase. Keeping the thugs in range, we ripped onto Interlagos expressway, then onto a dark road loaded with potholes. We raced after them, burning rubber on the curves, turning right, then left, finally ending up in a nearly deserted area, with hardly any houses and several empty lots. We started up a steep street. It was bordered by a wall, a fucking mess, with huge cracks and chipped plaster.

"Grab the shotgun from the back seat!" Bellochio yelled.

I took the 12 gauge and got ready to fire, leaning half my body out the window, waiting for my chance to take a shot. When we were about ten meters from the Audi, I aimed and fired. Since the car was jumping around like a colt, I only hit one of the streetlights. I took another shot, and this time I hit one of the tires. Out of control, the Audi slammed into the wall. The doors opened and three men escaped, almost at the same time. One took off down the street and the other two scaled the wall.

"You go for the guy on the street!" I yelled to Bellochio, as I grabbed a flashlight from the glove compartment and tore out of the car.

He took off in the squad car. It wasn't long before I heard the screeching breaks and Bellochio bellowing, "Hold it right there, you son-of-a-bitch!"

I went up to the Audi, turned on the inside light, and saw a body collapsed on the back seat, the head dripping with blood. It was either my shot or Bellochio's. Later we'd draw straws. I left the Audi and started to climb the wall. I was so out of shape it practically killed me. I got all banged up and, when I fell down on the other side, I almost landed in a pile of garbage. Leftovers from a construction sight, metal tables and chairs broken into pieces, rotten mattresses, all piled up. There were a bunch of trees and brush beyond that, where the hoodlums were hiding. You could hear noises. They were trying to escape. I wasted no time heading out after them. Then I heard a thud and a scream. I got there just in time to see, by the light of the flashlight, a man on his knees with his hands up, begging me, "For the love of God, don't shoot!"

He must have tripped on a branch or some rocks and lost his weapon. That's why he was on his knees, begging. Without letting the son-of-a-bitch out of my sight I held the light to the brush until I found the weapon in the middle of some grass. I grabbed his pistol, walked over to him, and bashed him on the head. There was still the other guy, who might be trying to scale the wall across the empty lot, or else be trying to take a shot at me. As a precaution, I turned off the flashlight. I found my way by the light of the moon and by the sound of his running. But at one point everything was still. I hid behind a bush and waited. Suddenly I heard a sound on my left. By the moonlight, I saw a piece of shiny metal. Without thinking twice I shot. I heard a muffled cry, turned on my flashlight and ran toward it. Behind a bunch of weeds, I came across a kid lying on the ground. He was trembling, his hands on his stomach. Next to him there was a piece of something silvery. It was probably a leg broken off from an old metal chair. Why? To this day I can't explain it. Maybe to try in vain to defend himself from me? I flashed the light on the boy's face. He was sweating, his huge eyes were looking around, terrified, and he was shivering all over, as if he had a fever. He was probably no more than sixteen or seventeen.

"I don' wanna die . . . " he blubbered.

"You're not going to die," I told him, kneeling down and trying to determine the extent of the injury. A shot from a .38 usually does serious damage. Especially in the gut.

Just then I heard footsteps coming from behind and Bellochio's voice.

"What's up partner? Everything all right?"

"More or less," I said, miserably.

"What do you mean more or less? I tripped over some clown getting over here. I've got him handcuffed."

"The kid here is losing a lot of blood."

He leaned over with his flashlight to examine the wound. He looked at me, shaking his head.

"The ambulance is already on its way. I had to run over that idiot. So they can take the kid too. Although. . . . "

I held the light to the boy's face again. He wasn't shaking anymore. There was bloody slobber running down the corner of his mouth. Just because of the glint of a damned piece of metal, I thought sadly. A life taken for a glint in the dark. We went back to the street, dragging the handcuffed man. It wasn't long before we heard a siren. It was the ambulance. Then another squad car. Later, the police paramedics. We went back to the police station and wrote up the report. Armed robbery, followed by death.

As we left the Station, Bellochio, noticing I was upset, patted me on the back.

"It was either him or you, partner."

"A kid, Bellochio, no more than seventeen."

He shook his head.

"If someone's got to die, it should be my father, he's so old . . . Anyway," he concluded, "I think we need to water down the old gullet. Let's get some drinks, partner."

We stopped at some joint on Sabará avenue, near Bellochio's house. The beers came, but didn't go down very well. Bellochio was sitting there next to me, trying in vain to console me.

"Come on, man, aren't you going to tell me about that hot manager at the Bradesco Bank? She was calling you all day yesterday."

I really didn't feel like talking. Especially not about women. But I didn't want to piss him off. I started telling him about the Bradesco manager. But with so little gusto that he refilled my glass, shaking his head.

"Yeah, partner, one more shitty day."

"You can say that again."

The memory of the boy blubbering, saying he didn't want to die, came back to torture me. I looked at myself in the filthy mirror behind the bar. What I saw was a face so sad I felt like crying.

I pulled myself together, gnawed my lip and, unwillingly, I said:

"If you've gotta know, the babe's great in the sack."
Bellochio beamed.

"Hey, man! You don't mean you . . . ?"

I forced a smile and shrugged.

Bellochio said, "You son of a bitch, you don't waste
any time, do you?" He gulped down the rest of his beer
in one slug, "Whew. . . . that girl's sure got a great pair of
thighs! And tits! One time I was at Bradesco taking care
of some business and she came over to talk to me. I nearly
lost my mind."

He gave me a whack on the shoulder, "But I know she's
way too much for the likes of me," he said admiringly and
without a trace of envy, which was just like him. "But she
sure isn't too much for you, partner. . . . ."

For me . . . if he only knew what a pile of shit I was . . .
a real loser. I was heading down Avenida 23 de Maio,
toward downtown. I didn't want to go home. I didn't
want to stay out. I don't think I wanted to be anywhere.
I wanted to vanish from myself. And the boy's face kept
following me. In the shadows of the trees. Between
buildings. Mixed up with the street people sleeping under
bridges.

I got home, and went straight to the bathroom. I lifted
the top of the can and started retching. I heaved my guts
out. Then I sat there on the floor, with my head between
my arms and bawled. I bawled so hard I got a headache.
I got under the shower, but even the cold water didn't
help much. The back of my neck was throbbing. I got out,
looked for some aspirin, and couldn't find a thing. I sure
as hell didn't feel like going out in search of a pharmacy. I
lay down on the couch with a cold towel on my head. All

of a sudden I was gone. And I had the nightmare, "I don' wanna die . . . " the boy blubbered, and I put my hand on his stomach. His guts squirmed out of the bullet hole like maggots, along with worms and rot. I woke up soaked in sweat. Just a kid. Dead because of a damned piece of shiny metal. And that image has never left my mind.

Translated by K.C.S. Sotelino

Chilly Night

Fernando Bonassi

IN THE CHILLY NIGHT, policemen are flooding our Mooca neighborhood with the lights of a Cobra chopper. We now have a criminal in every tree and every drainpipe. As it crosses the shutters, the helicopter beam makes my shadow circle the room and return to my body. You can hear the neighbors panting as they peek through bathroom windows. All the while, the roofs of the buildings

---

FERNANDO BONASSI was born in 1962 in Mooca, the working class neighborhood of São Paulo described in his minimalist flash fiction included in this anthology. He has written collections of short stories, *Passaporte (Passport)* and *O Amor em Chamas (Love in Flames)*; novels, *Suburbio (Suburb)* and *O Pequeno Fascista (The Little Fascist)*; eight plays, including three dramatic monologues; and ten film scripts, including *Carandiru* and *Cabra-Cega (Blindman's Buff)*. He has also directed six short films. For the last ten years he has been a columnist for the prestigious *Folha de São Paulo*. In 1998 he won a fellowship in creative writing and spent the year in Berlin writing the collection of short stories *O Livro da Vida (The Book of Life)*. His stories have been published in German, French, and English.

keep flashing on and off. Now that rush hour is over, loco-
motives are hauling hundreds of tons of grain through the
streets of our district, almost silently. In the chilly night,
in the door of the Cobra, a policeman hugs his shotgun
and shoots anything that moves.

Translated by Luiza Franco Moreira

Taxi

Luiz Ruffato

ANY SPECIAL ROUTE YOU'D LIKE, SIR? No? Then
let's take the quickest. Which isn't the shortest, you know.
Here in São Paulo the shortest way isn't always the quickest. At this hour . . . quarter past five . . . at this hour the
city's grinding to a halt . . . the ring roads, the side streets,
the crossroads, the avenues, the streets, the lanes, the

Born in 1961 in Minas Gerais, LUIZ RUFFATO is known
for his fresh approach to storytelling and unique use of language. Many of his characters hail from the Brazilian working
class and boast highly distinctive voices. His short stories have
appeared in magazines and anthologies in the United States,
France, Italy, Uruguay, Argentina, Portugal, and Croatia. He
has written a novel, *De mim já nem se lembra* (*No One Remem-
bers Me Any More*), and several volumes of short stories. The
breathless monologue "Taxi" is an excerpt from *Eles eram mui-
tos cavalos* (*Many Many Horses*), which Ruffato himself humor-
ously refers to as a "literary installation." Heralded as one of
the most innovative works of fiction in Brazil, this collection
of interwoven stories has been published in Italy, France, and
Portugal and has been adapted to the stage.

---

alleys, everything, all clogged up with cars and horns. You know I once dreamed that the city stopped? I mean really stopped, completely. A huge traffic jam, a monster gridlock, like never before, and nobody could move an inch . . . It's like something out of a movie, isn't it? I like it. I like watching movies. But I prefer the oldies. Sometimes they show them on TV. There were some damned good actors back then, Tyrone Power, Burt Lancaster . . . My favorite's Victor Mature, know him? He was in that "Sons of Hercules" series, remember? Pretty damned good . . . There's a portrait of him on our living room wall. Well, not a portrait, it's a picture from a magazine that the missus cut out and had framed. You know what women are like . . . She knew I was a fan of Victor Mature's and wanted to do something nice for me . . . She gave it to me for my birthday . . . years ago. She hung it on the living room wall . . . And do you think I've got the courage to take it down? No sir. Would you, sir? One time, I was at home alone and I threw it on the floor. The glass broke to bits. I told her it was the wind and she believed me. I thought I'd seen the last of it. But what do you know, the next week there he was hanging on the wall again, spanking new, can you believe it, sir? She thinks I like it. What can I do? When my girls were teenagers—they're all married now, and happily married, thank God—they were real embarrassed by it. Dad, it's so tacky! they used to say. Their friends used to wonder if he was a relative. Who's the stud? they'd ask. I thought the girls had something there. It was ridiculous! I had a chat with the missus and she said, For heaven's sake, Claudionor! That's me, Claudionor. For heaven's sake,

Claudionor! They'll be leaving home soon and it'll be just
the two of us, old folks. You like the picture, so it's staying
where it is . . . So, in a nutshell, if you ever come to my
place, you'll see Victor Mature hanging on—the living
room wall! We even had a dog once, a fox terrier, and that
son-of-a-gun didn't leave a thing standing. He'd come
racing in the living room door and fly out the kitchen
door, that crazy tail of his knocking everything over,
vases, potted ferns, pesky kids. He even managed to
knock down an empty Danish cookie tin we kept on top
of the cupboard and put a dent in it, the devil. The wife
had a fit, because it was her piggy bank . . . She's a seamstress. She used it as a hiding place for the money she
made stitching hems, sewing buttons on shirts, taking in
pants, mending tears . . . But would you believe it, sir? He
never knocked down that damned picture! What can you
do? But anyway, the best movies for me are the old ones.
Movies today are all blood and guts . . . Nothing but violence . . . Excuse the language but there's someone screw-
ing in every scene! It's unbelievable! You go into the video
rental store and there's a shelf full of pornos. Some'll
make your hair stand on end! Women with women,
women with horses, yes sir, with horses! Women with
dogs, women with a whole bunch of men, for crying out
loud! I know because, just between you and me, we're all
God's children and once the missus took a trip down to
the beach, to our son-in-law's house, and I rented one . . .
I couldn't even watch it to the end it was such an unholy
mess. That stuff's pretty sick, huh? It's disgusting. I mean,
does anyone actually get off on it? You'd have to have
some kind of problem, for Chrissake! That was the first

and last time I ever rented one of those things. Nowadays, when the wife goes to the beach, I go with her. The house my son-in-law built down in Praia Grande is nice, roomy, smack on the beach. And to think he practically built it on his own! He's an offset operator over at the *Estadão* newspaper and bought the land back when he was single. In those days there were chickens in the streets, can you believe it? Chickens! He didn't have any money, so he built a concrete wall around the plot and slowly started laying the foundations, putting up the sides. When he got engaged to Maria Lúcia, he sped things up. He'd go down every weekend. Everything just as he liked it, from the pieces of broken glass on top of the outside wall to the colonial-style roof, from the slate floor to the color of the bathroom tiles. What an eye for detail. You've got to see it to believe it! And what a good guy! Just because he's doing well for himself, doesn't mean he's forgotten who his friends are. The house isn't just for him, it's for the relatives: all the in-laws, parents, brothers and sisters, friends . . . Every weekend there's someone down there firing up a steak on the barbecue. Everyone getting along just fine. You can bet your bottom dollar: go there any Saturday, and someone'll be there. The families are real tight-knit. Which is actually a good thing, cause my own family and my missus' family aren't like that. I left home real early, when I was still a boy. I rode down from up north on the back of a truck. If you could only have seen it . . . An old rattletrap with a tarp over it, a few planks of wood across the back for seats, my things in a knapsack, getting by on the food I'd packed, days and days on the road, good God! But I can't complain. São Paulo's been like a mother to me. As soon as I got here I found work. I got a job as a cleaner at an auto parts store in Santo André. Then I worked my way up, because that's how it was back then. If you were a hard worker, you had it all, not like now, it's kinda sad, there's no jobs for anyone. Look at me, I've still got a few years left in me, I'm retired, but I still have to rustle up some odd jobs, 'cause nobody gives a damn about old folks. Or young folks who've never had a real job, or any experience. And no one gives them a chance! How are these kids supposed to get any damned experience if they never get that first job? Back then they were so short of labor that as soon as we hopped off the truck, we were at work. They taught us on the job. I actually made some good money. More than once I took the missus to visit my old stompin' ground, Nossa Senhora das Dores, in the backlands of Sergipe. You've probably never heard of it. Once I took the whole family, six of us packed into the brand-new beetle I'd just bought. We got onto the Rio-Bahia Highway and off we went. The girls were already pretty big then, and the missus was all queasy, greenish. She's always been like that. It starts the minute she gets in a car. Now she's got herself a trick. She sniffs citron as she goes. She's fine from here to the beach, but back then it was pandemonium. What a stink! The girls haven't been back since . . . It makes me sad, I gotta tell you, sir. After all, it's my roots. But I get it. I'm no fool. There's nothing in that backwater for them. Me neither, to be honest. Most of my childhood friends, the folks I used to know, don't live there any more. The old folks are all dead. All we've got left is memory, but what exactly is that? We came back from that trip down High-

way 101. The girls loved it, of course, because we followed
the coast. We stopped in Guarapari. They've got this
black sand there, real good for rheumatism. The missus
had some pain in her joints that wouldn't go away, not
even with infiltration, so she'd cover herself in the sand,
just her face sticking out . . . And since I had nothing to
do, I'd head off to a bar. Maria Perpétua, my oldest, was
already old enough to take care of her brothers and sisters,
so I'd sit there looking out over the beach like a lord, a
bottle of beer and some fish sticks, and I'd sit there checking out the girls in bikinis who went past. I used to run
around a bit. Young guy, good-looking, a talker . . . There
wasn't a week when I didn't go out with a different woman.
And I'm not talking about the ones you pay, no sir, because
that's something I've never liked. If a woman wants to go
out with me, even today, she can't be looking to get something out of it, otherwise, I confess, I just can't do it.
Excuse the language, but I can't get it up. Back then I was
able to take a whole month's vacation, it was in my con-
tract. I had a house in Vila Nova Cachoeirinha, the kids
were still at home, but on the right path, the oldest, Maria
Perpétua, was studying to be a teacher . . . That's when I
slipped up . . . gave in to temptation . . . I got fired from
the firm I worked for and decided to use the money from
my payout to open a pinball parlor in my garage . . . You
won't believe what happened . . . I guess these things are
cursed. Doesn't matter what you do . . . To turn the
garage into a parlor I had to park my car out in the street.
I didn't have any insurance, just an iron steering-wheel
lock . . . And what do you know, the parlor turned into a
haunt for drug dealers, my car got stolen, and I went

bankrupt! In the blink of an eye, I had to get back up on my feet and start over . . . I got a job as a bus driver, scraped together some cash and my sons-in-law gave me a hand. I bought a taxi license, not this one, another one, for a spot over in Belém, then I got a spot in Lapa, a real good location . . .

But I've got two generations at home. My two oldest girls, Maria Perpétua and Maria do Carmo, had it better. They went to school, got degrees. Maria do Carmo's a big-time lawyer. She's got her own practice with a partner over in Horto. She's single, doing well for herself, and she's got a great apartment nearby. She's even been abroad, you know. She's got the travel bug. She's even been on a ship. I think she got her boldness from me . . . She gave me a photo of herself in the snow, in Bolivia. I just think she's kind of sad. She's never wanted to get married. I think she might've had her heart broken, I'm not sure . . . The missus has a cousin who when she found out her husband had another family, a wife and three kids, stopped eating, drinking, walking, everything. She wasted away, died a vegetable. Maria do Carmo's a different story. She's always been a private person, real quiet, so we never really know the whys and wherefores . . . Maria Perpétua got her degree in teaching. She's married, lives in Campo Limpo, teaches at a municipal school. She's doing well for herself, thank God. Her husband's in retail. Nice guy, a bit of a smooth talker, but in his business if you don't keep your wits about you, you don't last, isn't that right, sir? There's no two ways about it. But my other kids had a tougher time of it. Maria Lúcia and Pedro didn't get as far in their studies . . . But, thank God, it hasn't stopped them from doing OK. Maria Lúcia's married to the son-in-law who's got the place in Praia Grande. She's a housewife, only finished elementary school, but I guess she's better off than her sisters. Pedro's got a market stall. He sells bananas—did you know selling bananas at the market is a pretty good business? Pedro's fine, he's got a good house and his kids want for nothing, though he rides them hard. The oldest is thirteen and gets up before dawn on the weekends to help his dad. That boy's real smart. The other day . . . Oh, we're here . . . The other day he won a prize at school . . . No, no, just what's on the meter, not a cent more . . . That's my rule. There's colleagues out there who charge additional fees, fifty percent more if the passenger's a gringo, twenty percent more if they suspect they're from out of town . . . There's a name for that, in my opinion: dishonesty. Not me, I charge what's on the meter . . . But, just to finish, this kid, my grandson, João Paulo, the other day he won a math competition, would you believe it? Look, here's my card, sir. That's my cell phone number. If you need me, just call: Claudionor, at your disposal. Thank you very much and have a good trip. See you later!

Translated by Alison Entrekin

The Saint and the City

Benedicto Monteiro

"IN THE BEGINNING there was just an image, a rough wooden image. The missionaries who came to conquer Amazônia had it among their belongings."

Even today, nobody understands why those missionaries chose that spot for the new city. Perhaps it appeared to them at that instant as the highest spot in the immense flooded plain—the firmest shore, the densest forest, the safest shelter, or the most favorable climate.

Early on they understood that they had settled in the

BENEDICTO MONTEIRO (1924–2008), in his tetralogy *Verde Vagomundo, O Minossauro, A Terceira Margem*, and *Aquele Um*, created the most vivid depiction we have of Amazônia, the fluvial civilization on the Amazonian river system. *Verde Vagomundo* is not confined to nature, however, but reveals the author's reaction to his imprisonment and loss of political rights at the hands of the Brazilian military dictatorship (1964–1985). The novel revolves around the feast of the patron saint of the village of Alenquer, Saint Anthony. This is the first publication in English translation of any of Monteiro's work.

middle of an intricate, liquid, green labyrinth. The lake, which in early winter seemed to have a definite shape, with plants growing on permanent shores, little by little devoured those banks, flooding everything in a radius that nobody could measure or take in visually.

The strip of land where they had set up their camp at the height of the rains ended up pressed between the flood waters and the dense virgin jungle. They couldn't walk, but they could navigate all roads in all directions. All they had to do was fell a tree, carve it out, caulk the gaps, and the water would take charge of bobbing it through the jungle and over the fields.

Months later, the dry summer season came just to show the careless missionaries that that landscape, so pretty in winter, didn't have permanent outlines. As soon as the water stopped falling from the sky, as if by a spell, it also began disappearing from the hollows in the earth. It's true, the sky remained blue, with rare white clouds rent by the wind. But the vegetation was stained in colors and shadows ranging from black-green to the color of dry dirty straw, rotten branches, and twisted tree trunks.

Dried-out grasses crept over the cracked, parched land, which seemed to become more tepid and muddy each day. What was green on those waters became bagasse pierced by sticks, or even rotten grass covering the soft, dirty mud of the ravines. The trees showed all their roots on the promontories of the high banks. Water was almost mud, the lake an immense swamp, and the plants an endless floodplain.

When the surface of the water became so dirty it no longer reflected the sky, the rough wooden image disappeared from the sanctuary. There was the greatest agitation, and a wave of fear and hope spread over the entire small settlement that surrounded the little chapel that had just been raised at the center of the encampment.

The news spread as if it were a miracle, but the missionaries were troubled when they found that the image had disappeared mysteriously. They immediately sought to blame certain people who spoke openly about moving; they searched houses for any clues to the unexplained and complicated disappearance.

In the midst of that distrust, everyone went through famine, privation, and great need. There were many disagreements among the inhabitants. Until the winter rains came again, everything that happened in the settlement was tied to the disappearance of Saint Anthony's image. "Saint Anthony is showing us that we should leave this terrible labyrinth as soon as possible," said some. "It's a divine miracle of the holy image," said others. "What we should do is get out of this hole immediately," many hazarded. "I wish! If we could at least be closer to the banks of the Amazon," thought almost everyone.

It was nevertheless a modest explorer who wasn't even thinking about winter or summer or even about the miracle who found the image of the so eagerly sought Saint Anthony on an ordinary tree trunk on the bank of a distant side channel of the river, lost at the limits of the horizon.

There was no measure to determine, in terms of number and size, an idea of the distances. The explorer, although he could give a minutely detailed description of the jungle and the plants species, could add nothing other than that the image had been found on the trunk of a tree, and on the bank of a distant long, sinuous bayou. Days, nights, moons, leagues, and distances separated that tortuous oceanlike river from the small, recently established settlement. Lakes, bayous, channels, jungles, fields, and floodplains made up the long and difficult road back.

But when the image reappeared in the chapel, there was a great celebration, and everyone knew a miracle had occurred. The missionaries prayed, but they also took other measures. They put locks on the chapel doors and glass in the sanctuary doors. The inhabitants received as a gift everything that the winter rains brought them, with the waters traveling freely over the fields and reaching all the recesses of the jungle.

A new summer arrived and surrounded the settlement with mud. This time, almost all the fish died in the pools that remained in the lowlands. Hunger once again hounded that small corralled population. The grasses dried, and even a forest fire started. And Saint Anthony, in the middle of all these misfortunes, disappeared again. Again the missionaries accused some directly. They searched the suspects' houses and invoked divine retribution on the unfaithful. But in the middle of that small population the idea of a miracle grew. It was a true miracle.

So an expedition was organized to search that immense green horizon for the holy image. And to the fear of all, Saint Anthony was found on the trunk of the same tree in the very same bayou.

Whenever the summer turned harsh, Saint Anthony's image would disappear from the chapel. And the population became more convinced that the saint, via the miracle, was showing them where to move.

The rains had already stopped and the waters were revealing the shores when the only missionary left in the

AMAZON 99

settlement called on all the settlers to repent. He told the
faithful of the congregation that they were victims of a
terrible trick and that they had naturally fallen into the
sin of a contaminating heresy: the periodic disappearance, for unknown reasons, of Saint Anthony's image
from the site chosen for that settlement. That was why
the missionary had gathered the faithful and begun that
novena. God would receive their fervent prayers and show
through His divine grace that nothing good was built
without sacrifice. That settlement, in the middle of that
terrible labyrinth, was one more witness to the unshak-
able faith of Christians in God's great wisdom.

"What about Saint Anthony?" shouted a voice among
the penitents.

"Saint Anthony," replied the missionary, "was also a
faithful disciple of Christ, who lived his entire life on
Earth being put to the greatest tests." And he continued
preaching obedience, devotion, and penitence. He concluded by saying that he couldn't continue serving the
aims of the unhappy.

On the ninth day of repentance, before all the settlement's inhabitants, the missionary preached an eloquent
sermon calling for faith and spiritual sacrifice by all the
faithful. He felt that, with that spiritual preparation,
the population would be properly catechized to face the
effects of the upcoming summer. The novena should at
least lessen the agonizing expectations of the entire population at the foreboding signs of the distressing difficulties of the worst summer.

But to prevent Saint Anthony's image from being
kidnapped and taken to another place, the missionary

announced the measures he would take. He didn't fail to explain carefully to the faithful that those measures, which he thought absolutely necessary although they might appear disrespectful of the saint, were, nevertheless, the result of long nights of vigils during which he prayed for divine inspiration . . . and even the grace of a miracle. . . . But . . .

They had somehow to tie Saint Anthony's image to the altar.

A loud and endless murmuring was the only reaction from the faithful. And even today, it isn't known whether or not there was agreement among the inhabitants for Saint Anthony to remain tied up during the summer that threatened to be so harrowing.

What is known is that, from the immense and endless murmuring, a heated discussion arose among the people to determine what type of rope would be used to tie up the beloved saint. Some thought that the ropes used for the sacred task should be woven of *embira*, a fiber derived from the *mungubeira*, or silk-cotton tree, the tree on whose trunk the fugitive saint was always found. Besides, the *mungubeira* was the first tree to announce the receding of the flood. It was enough for its ripe fruit to burst on the branches and its red shells to fall like small canoes in the flowing water for the level of the lake to begin dropping. Not satisfied with the announcement made in the waters, the *mungubeira* displayed another sign of receding waters: if the red shells of the mature fruit sank or ran aground in still waters, the seed vessels, freed from the ripe fruit, traveled far—they filled the sky with a flock of white flakes. Nobody could stop these flakes, because they spread in all directions and at the whim of the wind. But, many thought, ropes woven of *embira* would not work to tie up the saint. Perhaps ropes woven of *piçaba* would work. This was a spiny fiber of a wild palm that could well symbolize the intention of sacrifice. Others argued for *tucum*, *curu*, *curuá*, or *curauá*, or strong Manila ropes.

Nevertheless, the will and diligence of the pious ladies prevailed. During the nights of penitence, they silently wove holy ropes from multicolored silk cords and ribbons.

So Saint Anthony was closed up in a bell jar and carefully tied to the altar's pillars with the soft, colored ropes.

After all these measures, only a miracle itself, a true miracle, could bring about the now-customary disappearance.

People began to look insistently at the sky: it was pure blue and blinding. They felt restless and terrified because the waters flowed more and more slowly and were muddier and muddier. The wind blew as from a huge furnace. The sun broke abruptly into dawn and stubbornly invaded the edge of night. There was no longer morning or a transition in the evening; there was only day and night. Shadows were already shadows and colors also fulgently changed color. Only green multiplied into a thousand tones. But in spite of it all, Saint Anthony remained impassively in the bell jar secured to the altar.

It was at night, late at night, when a sharp blow on the chapel bell startled the population. Before the last peal of the bell had echoed through the jungle, nobody took the initiative to approach the bell tower.

Candles, oil lamps, candleholders, beams of light appeared at doorways, windows, cracks in walls and everyone started to move about. All the light beams projected over the clearing where the tiny chapel was, but nobody had the courage to break through that illuminated boundary in the night, as if the light unexpectedly fenced off sound, fire against the darkness that encircled the settlement, the uncertainty of faith against the miracle. But in those first moments, everyone remained motionless, at the edge of the shadows, pressured by a funereal silence.

In the midst of that waiting, someone remembered the missionary. The priest's house was closed up without a glint of light. The torches that were contained by the contours of windows and doors and made points of light in the middle of the wild jungle fields began anew to move in various directions. They lighted up, went out, softened, ran, ran in beams of light over the land, climbed trees, divided at tree branches, split on roads, sparkled, reflected on leaves, penetrated the cracks in walls, made shadows, improvised a thousand contours, and disappeared only in the breadth of the black sky.

The missionary was finally awakened and wrapped in the light of the torches, and he had to face, at that hour of the night, the anguished eyes of all his faithful. They all wanted to know why the bell had rung. And where was the saint. Yes, the saint. The tolling of the bell must be notice of a miracle. The miracle of the flight had a sound now. Light and sound. All that was lacking was the presence, the presence of the image. They all ran to the chapel. The chapel was open. What about the saint? The saint was simply not there. The sanctuary remained closed. The glass dome was intact. And the ropes woven of silk and ribbons were scattered on the floor.

"Let's go, people, after Saint Anthony."

That was the order. Who gave it, where it came from, nobody knows, even today. From then on all that was heard was the noise of the bell, the uproar of motion in the shadowy dance and in the movement of the torches and firebrands.

If there were in the world a fairy fest, a battle of shadows, it could be that it took place the night of that precipitous move. The effects attained even today on stages and movies with ghosts, windows, fairies, witches, medieval castles, and flights of stairs pale before the rhythm, tones and overtones, contours, plastic effects of that spectacle. Suffice it to say that everything occurred on the shore of a muddy lake in the middle of a black, virgin jungle.

When a woman ran carrying a straw basket, a man carrying a chest, a child pulling a dog, nobody could imagine the kinds of shadows projected on the ground, in the trees, on the walls, and even reaching into the black waters of the lake. A pole, a hamper, a fishing net, a child, a useless cart wheel, men carrying a canoe on their shoulders became unforeseeable dynamic figures projected onto the blackness of the night. Yes, in spite of the firebrands, torches, lanterns, candlesticks, and lamps, it was night! Night-night. Night in the almost stagnant mud of the lake. And the sky above the last brightness over the forest. In the forest, there was a dance, a battle, a phantasmagorical representation where light and shadow gave form and deformity to everyone. Sometimes the light beams on the ground were lost in the darkness. Sometimes they climbed up tree trunks, ran, ran up tree branches, trembled on the leaves, and got lost in the sky or stagnated in the lake.

The only clear image in all that hubbub was the shadow of the priest projected by all the torches and firebrands. In his anxiousness to contain that impulse to move, he first opened his arms, and then the torches projected his shadow as a large cross on the wall of the chapel.

They had to tie the poor missionary to the crossbeam of the bell tower while the women gathered the liturgical vestments. The saint's altar was disassembled and transported, as a candlestick found paths in the darkness. And they only freed the fearful priest when they were all on board the cluttered canoes and ready to depart.

They still tell how, in the middle of the lake, in the deepest darkness, canoes ran aground and stuck in the mud, causing a terrible panic. Since there wasn't really anybody in charge, in the middle of the journey and as a result of the panic, the priest's authority was reestablished. They say it was hard for him to gather the canoes that were aground, half-flooded, and dispersed. They were all completely disoriented, sailing in the mud and the almost complete darkness.

Then there was a terrible heavy silence. The missionary took advantage of that silence to recommend that they all stay where they were, quiet in their canoes, until morning dawned on the horizon. But the darkness was so dark that nobody could calculate where the horizon might be. The lake was completely still, the black night weighed on the mud so that there were no reflections. But any motion made waves in those waters. Waters that were mud. Because of the silence and the mud, the night was a deeper night.

Everyone who was waiting for the light to rend that dark veil was surprised by the gap opened by the shout.

Lots of shouts, grunts, horrible grunts, irreconcilable grunts, mixed with the sound of the muddy water and was softened by the darkness of the night. They immediately thought it must be the big snake, the mother-of-the-lake, the mythological boat-sinking snake, the *boiúna*, or even the enchanted thousand-headed monster.

It was the clacking of jawbones and the hoarse half-drowned grunt that revealed to the more knowledgeable a great pack of hogs. During the summer, the feral hogs migrated in large, disoriented packs from solid ground out to the river's edge. This was, certainly, a fierce migrating pack that had lost its way and taken a wrong turn.

Today, the refugees' experiences—struggling against the mud, struggling against the night, and, finally, having to witness, motionless and appalled, the crazed passing of the frenetic hogs—cannot be described.

Those who escaped and reached that sinuous bayou found the image of Saint Anthony on a tree trunk.

He was in a kind of a niche carved into an ordinary trunk on the banks of the narrow bayou, which, after it ran over islands, swamps, jungle, fields, and endless floodplains, finally and still far off perhaps emptied into the Amazon, but which, after forming islands, creating swamps, watering vegetation, could die in a lake or hide itself in the deep jungle.

There, in that spot, on top of the trunk of that tree, they built the new chapel and founded the new city.

Translated by Albert Bork

Sunset

Benedicto Monteiro

I THOUGHT THAT, when the sun went down, night would fall suddenly and completely. Total mistake: it's not like that in Amazônia. It's not like that on a lake that defines the horizon with a line of water.

There's always a struggle between the almost-still water and the clouded sky, between the reflected light and night shadow. Because the light is only distantly filtered rays, shadow frames everything. In Amazônia it seems that night floats in the depths of the waters and is born in the jungle's entrails. The lake is like that; it is water itself. A cloud is a cloud, and the sky is an unstable blue. Only shadow is pure absence and pure distance. In this transition of time, of things and colors, the water is almost dead. Shadow-water, cloud-water, cloud-wave-water, slight-cloud-wave-water, light-water-light, reflected-light-water, diffuse-light-water, soft-light-water, light-arrow-water, dispersed-light-water, ceasing-light-water, water-colored-water, cloud-colored-water, distant-sky-water, mirror-

This is excerpted from *Verde vagomundo* and is Monteiro's second piece in this collection. See page 95 for his biographical information.

water, mirror-like-water, shattered-sometimes-adjustable-mirror-water, mirror-red-water, copper-red-mirror-water, steel-red-mirror water, blood-red-water, rubicund-red-mirror-water, red-fading-blood-water, silver-red-water, water-mirror-red-water, gold-red-water, gold-water, golden-water, red-gilded-water, reflected-gilded-water, reverberating-sky-water, dissipating-cloud-water, disappearing-cloud-water, dark-eddy-water, muggy-warm-water, lake-water, water-lake, mirror-space-lake-water, water reflecting-distant-sky, distant water, sky-dived-into the lake, cloud-cloud, white-cloud, heron-cloud, seagull-flock-cloud, veil-cloud, cloak-cloud, holy-saint-cloak-cloud, gauze-cloud, damn-fluttering-cloud, wandering-cloud, flying-carpet-nest-cloud, diaphanous-patina-cloud, shaft-cloud, dart-cloud, cloud-filtering-arrow-light, open-void-cloud, open-void-cloud-to allow-dart-light-to pass, greyhound-cloud, avian cloud, image-cloud, bird-cloud, dragon-bird-winged-horse-dragon-cloud, swan-and-fish-cloud, bird-flock-pack-of-dogs-airplane-cloud, flash-cloud, lightning-bolt-cloud, foundry-cloud, pig-iron-ignited-steel-foundry-cloud, trail-cloud, comet-tail-cloud, rocket-fire-dart-sword-cloud, cloud-cloud, enigma-cloud, blue-cloud, distant-sky-blue-cloud, blue-blue, pure-sky-blue, sun-blue, galaxy-sun-blue, distant-distances-blue, blue-halo-blue, almost-reflected-blue, blue-ray-blue, wandering-blue, absent-blue, blue-turning-white, blue-turning-ash, blue-turning-to-shadow, shadow-blue, blue-of-blue-shadow, shadow-almost-shadow, shadow-in-water, shadow-shadow. No color in space. Night arrived through the water.

Translated by Albert Bork

Claws Revealed

by Astrid Cabral

DONA DADÁ, our new neighbor, came to Manaus from the backwoods of Manacapuru accompanied by numerous trunks, furniture, a black dog, and a pet tortoise. She seemed like a serious, reliable person. However, we quickly saw that we were wrong. In fact, she was cold and austere, which is not the same thing. She would bellow at the servant girls who worked for her and who always looked downcast, frightened by her reprimands.

ASTRID CABRAL is best known for poetry and is the prize-winning author of ten volumes. Her first book, *Alameda,* published in 1963, is a collection of boldly imaginative stories dealing with the secret life of plants. Despite having lived for decades in Rio and having spent years abroad, the Amazon of her roots has not abandoned her, as in this narrative set in the Manaus of the forties, where the life of humans seems emotionally intertwined with that of animals. Turning her back on previous flights of fancy, Cabral returns with bruising realism, devoid of moralizing, to the arduous difficulties of social coexistence and the harm that may result from its conflicts.

Her face in a frown, she never smiled. We suspected that she didn't have a single tooth in her mouth, because of her muddled speech. It could hardly be understood.

"Nuffa yu ruckus. Shut yu yap, yu gaddam brats. Naptime ri'now."

She had a face as round as a saucer and a hard stare. And a certain affectation as well, from the ringlets she wore, one on each side of her head. Besides being unpleasant, she was lazy. She spent hour after hour installed at the window, keeping a sharp eye on the street, her soft flabby arms leaning on a red cushion. She made a point of exhibiting her collection of rings. But in showing off all those gems and gold, she also revealed her filthy nails where dirt had embedded a black line.

Bit by bit she began to reveal other claws, as well.

First it was the mangoes and the guavas that began to disappear from our yard. My sisters and I began to notice that the fruit would mature, only to disappear as by a stroke of magic, just when they were at their ripest. No rain had fallen to knock them from the trees and no one told us of any kids sneaking around, or ravening parrots or monkeys playing in the yard. We imagined it was the cunning of starving bats that came at night while we were asleep.

Until one moonlit night we saw protruding over the fence a forked stick with a basket hanging from the end, shaking the branch from which a ripe mango was hanging. We were startled by that distant vision. Could it be the workings of a ghost? One of those souls in agony we had heard so much about? We stayed silent, stock still and on the look-out, until everything returned to immobility after the pole, coming forth from the vegetation, leaned itself up against the wall of Dona Dadá's house.

One Saturday, the cook at our house came to tell Grandma she couldn't have the chicken ready for the Sunday lunch. It had escaped, it really had, she had already searched the entire backyard. Grandma just said, "What are you talking about, Luzia? Chickens don't fly. I bought the poor things with their wings cut."

But there was nothing to be done and soon others began to disappear. Today it would be the red Plymouth Rock, a few days later it would be the already fattened bantams recently bought at market.

And then, early one morning, while it was still half-dark, Luzia happened to see a shape spreading corn in a corner by the fence. Later on, sweeping up the yard, she found the wire of the fence lifted up out of place. Quickly, she thought, it's through here they're escaping. She began to look more carefully at the neighboring yard and noticed that amongst Dona Dadá's poultry there were a lot of hens with featherless necks. Except for the two Angolas, the others were plucked bald. Looking more closely, she was able to recognize four of them, a white one and three red ones that had disappeared from this side and now were over there, all with featherless necks.

Luzia told us of her discovery. We considered it an outrage. For us, a thief was a being without a face, a being so well hidden that no one could lay eyes on him. But now, there it was, right under our nose, that lady well known to all of us. For certain she had ordered her poor serving girls to carry out those actions.

We put together a plan. The first time we saw Dona

Dadá going out with her husband, all dressed up for Sunday Mass, we went to ask permission to go and get our chickens, which had fled through the break in the fence. Said and done. We played innocent and said, "Good morning, Doctor Nicolau, please allow us to go and get our chickens which ran into your yard."

He was an affable man, respected by all. He merely said, "First ask the servants to tie up the dog." Dona Dadá, arm in arm with Doctor Nicolau, gazed at us with a face scowling in hatred, but tight as a clam, not saying a word. We brought back three of our chickens, that's all we managed to recover, since all the others were already in the bellies of our neighbors.

Some time later, one of Grandpa's old cronies, come for a visit, asked, "Did you eat it, my old friend, was it good, that turtle I sent you for your birthday?" Grandpa was surprised. "What turtle, my friend?"

The old crony went to talk to the guy who was supposed to deliver the present and he said that when he arrived with the order, a fat woman in the window of the house next door had said, "Over here, boy, I been waitin' days for that little creature."

Our rage boiled over. To have to deal with shameless people is a hard thing to swallow. To complicate matters, Doctor Nicolau was a good man. He would put on parties for the young kids and he was even district judge. An important man, but without any silly pride. We felt sorry for him, poor victim of that false woman, that shrew.

The question now was to decide what lesson one could give that witch with a hidden broomstick. It would be hard to catch her with her hand in the jar. How could anyone excuse a woman of her standing and with so many rings for envying and coveting so much someone else's things?

Grandfather's rule was that you should never do what you have criticized others for doing. A simple question of consistency. But mother always thought that excessive tolerance only served to nourish error and that one would lose nothing by arranging for a lesson.

So, on the day that Dona Dadá's pet tortoise dug a hole like an armadillo and ended up in our yard next to the cherimoya tree, Mom didn't hesitate. She told Luzia to prepare it with all the usual seasonings, cilantro, fitweed, Murupi peppers, parsley, and scallions, and not to forget to accompany it with manioc flour, everything as in a true and festive turtle feast.

We ate without remorse and with pleasure, for justice had left our breasts washed clean. As if a cloud had been lifted. Not even Grandpa complained.

It would have been the perfect occasion to have Dona Dadá come searching for the creature, trying to stand up for him, so we could make a clean breast of it all, creating a climate of good neighbors and ending all resentments. But she didn't utter a peep. That time once again it was she who kept her mouth shut.

We made a racket throughout siesta time, a sign of our victory, a provocation.

Translated by Alexis Levitin

Truth Is a Seven-Headed Beast

Milton Hatoum

SHE WAS A SHADOW lost in a flooded world. We still don't know her name or where she lives. Some say the poor woman's from a hole in the wall in the ragged Colinas district; others have seen her roaming the alleys of the Céu neighborhood, and God only knows whether she's a daughter of the city or the jungle. They say she tried to check into Santa Casa Hospital, but the security guard shooed her away and she was caught in a fierce downpour

---

MILTON HATOUM, born in 1952 in Manaus, capital of the state of Amazonas, has taught at the University of the Amazon and at the University of California at Berkeley. Author of *The Brothers, Tale of a Certain Orient,* and *Ashes of the Amazon,* he has won the prestigious Jabuti Prize for best novel of the year twice. Of Lebanese descent, Hatoum is a principal voice both for the Amazon and for Brazil's far-flung Arab population. Much of his work is set in the surrealistic jungle capital of Manaus, and the action—imagined or real—takes place inside the splendidly eclectic and strangely misplaced Opera House, a grand reminder of the Amazon's late-19th century rubber boom.

---

in the middle of Praça São Sebastião. The church was closed, the square deserted, house fronts silent. Somehow it all seemed linked to the dread that comes with the December rainy season here in Manaus. She must have felt the first contractions as she wandered the square outside our majestic Opera House. We can imagine her eyes searching for someone to help her, but there was not a living soul in sight. Rather than struggling with the stairs, she dragged herself up the nearest ramp to the entrance, somehow managed to pull open the massive wooden doors, and crawled inside.

The Opera House was empty. Now and again a sudden flash of light would scratch the window and a rumble boom down from the sky like a warning. Hauling herself along, the woman plunged into a shadowy place where nothing—except her damp body and wet hair—recalled the wet tumult outside. She found herself in the Opera House auditorium, where a sloping aisle led her down near the stage. She lay down on the velvety red between the rows, waiting for the propitious moment to give birth.

Maybe it was the thunder's crack that broke the silence reigning over the refuge—no one knows for certain what set the chandeliers that dangled from the high dome to swaying. We do know, however, that the disturbance registered in a small attic room where, stretched in a hammock, the self-proclaimed watchman of the Opera House lay drifting far from the world. Álvaro Celestino de Matos—a taciturn 87-year-old with the accent of an immigrant from the Minho region of Portugal—woke with a start. There it was again—the strange noise he'd imagined he'd been dreaming—the *voice* of a singer from a distant night in childhood. He floated for a while in that shifting place where sleep and dream mysteriously merge, unsure whether what he heard was a product of the storm or of a certain Thursday in 1910: the famous day—still crystal in memory—when as a boy he had waxed and waxed the stage, lovingly preparing it to receive the precious feet of Angiolina Zanuchi, soprano.

Nothing, or almost nothing, had changed about his modest room since that day. Conspicuous on the wall beside the window was a photograph of the singer descending the gangplank of the Queen Elizabeth. But it was impossible to look at the photograph without also taking in the view out the window: a single church spire with a belfry and a bell as regular as the rain, until nightfall, when the silhouette of the church faded and a lunar disk appeared in the center of the window. These two images— the picture of the soprano and the profile of the Church of São Sebastião—were unalterably linked in both vision and memory. For how many years had he been gazing at them before sleep—sixty, seventy? He would drift off with those two images in his head; and on waking, the first thing he'd do was to light the kerosene lamp so that a flame lit up Angiolina's face beside the moon-flooded landscape.

Yesterday, when Seu Álvaro opened his eyes, the view from his window looked like an aquarium full of brownish water, and the contours of the singer's face had disappeared; only the broadside of the ship emerged from the murk of his attic room. The watchman wasn't sure in this lingering night whether the sound he heard was a human voice or the chords of a piano, but it no longer belonged to sleep or dream. It seemed to come from a long way off, probably from inside the Opera House, down below.

For a man approaching his nineties, the distance from the attic to the ground floor was practically an abyss. This did not discourage him. He decided to brave the journey armed with his Winchester, which had intimidated countless men and brought down countless animals in times past. Now, almost the same height as his stooped frame, the rifle served as a cane.

The descent was slow and arduous, but it wasn't fatigue that set him to shaking the moment he stepped onto the carpeted ground floor. Seu Álvaro realized that this sudden trembling had nothing to do with age; instinct told him that something ominous was about to happen this rainy morning. Was the half-open entryway door a sign of an intruder? He glanced out at the monument. Of the four bronze boats, only one was visible, seemingly adrift in the center of the square, and the wings of a submerged angel looked like an anchor floating free in space. Pushing the door fully open with the butt of the gun, the watchman noticed a red stain that trailed along the floor and disappeared into the auditorium. Choosing another route, he turned down one of the side corridors: a winding wall of doors that gave onto the main floor boxes. He had decided to slip into the seventh box and was already turning the doorknob when he heard the sound again— odder now, more threatening. And so he stood and waited a few seconds, and this moment of hesitation (the anxiety of an old man?) caused him to change his mind. Turning away from the door, a strange sensation led him to the backstage area. There he found a safe haven on the stage, with the painted canvas curtain separating him from the concert hall itself.

Wary but not unsteady—his past, his profession, and perhaps his rifle all helping to keep him calm—the watchman felt his way along the closest wall and found among the spider webs a wooden handle. He yanked it upward. A thread of light shot toward him through a hole in the curtain, which glowed with sudden brightness from the other side. The watchman could well envision the shapes and colors of the immense paintings now visible in the hall: herons and storks surrounded by white lilies and other aquatic flowers, and a water nymph reclining on a shell that floated atop the "Meeting of the Waters" of the Rio Negro and the Rio Amazonas. Seu Álvaro moved up to the curtain, bringing his right eye directly to the hole, and shivered when he realized that the ring of light coincided with the water nymph's outlined navel. Steadying himself on his rifle, he scanned the hall, searching for the source of the noise that had awoken him. It was disheartening, somehow, to find the hall deserted, chandeliers and upholstery dusty, plaster busts of Bach and Shubert—in past times honored by famous pianists—lusterless.

Today the hall looked utterly abandoned, the boxes empty . . . until that one wide-open eye detected a shadow—perhaps a body?—down front near the stage. For the first time the watchman was a little afraid. He put on his glasses, bringing the hall into a clearer focus: more of his old friends, busts of Carlos Gomes, Racine, and Moliere. And, there in a front row seat, the glistening body of a dark-haired woman.

The watchman lurched back from the curtain and

stood there, imagining the painting on the other side: the
water nymph lying on her shell, almost naked, a white and
luxuriant body accented by the light. Then he touched his
right hand to the curtain and gently caressed the nymph's
belly; the roughness of the canvas on his skin jolted him
into remembering that it really was a painting. He lined
his eye up with the hole in the curtain again: the woman
had crossed her legs. Her hair hung down over her breasts.
From this distance he couldn't make out the expression
on her face, but the eyes seemed large, almond-shaped
maybe. Her posture, demeanor? That body was simply
a body. Not more than twenty years old, he thought to
himself, as the woman leaned back in her chair, cradling
a baby in her arms. She enfolded the infant tenderly, and,
when she opened her mouth, he expected a voice or a
song; but it was merely a yawn. Then the woman began
licking the baby's face, her lips and tongue gleaming in
the light from the chandelier. As if in a dream, the hall
suddenly went black, just like that. The watchman closed
his eyes and struck the floor several times impatiently
with his rifle. As the noise echoed through the theater,
he guffawed once, then smiled at himself. Giving in fully
to laughter, he didn't notice the loss of his gun until he
staggered and fell to his knees. Two men dressed in white
dragged him downstage through the gloom and depos-
ited him in the middle of some old scenery: a small room
with wooden walls and a single window that framed a
church spire and belfry in a sky bright with tin foil stars,
with a cardboard moon hung in the air like a mobile. One
of the nurses flicked a light on and lunged at Seu Álvaro
when he tried to climb into the hammock that was part

of the old set. He was breathing heavily, his eyes never wavering from a certain spot on the curtain, as if to drill through to the front row seat just on the other side.

Night had fallen by the time they arrived at the Estrada de Flores Mental Hospital. We found him lying on a straw mattress. His hands were shaking badly, but on his wrinkled face he wore an enigmatic smile. Raspy-voiced and somber, he related what had happened yesterday morning in the Opera House. Dr. S. L., the psychiatrist on duty, stated that Senhor de Mato's declaration was consistent with that of a man who had for some time been suffering the swamp of senility. Before hospitalization, his nomad's life had followed the course of the seasons: in summer, dawn would find him in one of the bronze boats of the monument in the Praça São Sebastião, where he spent hours contemplating the statue of a woman. During the rainy season, he took refuge in the abandoned scenery of the Opera House, where he'd been found on several occasions, either singing or staring at one of the seats in the front of the hall.

One particular element in the former watchman's story caught our attention. In one of his pockets, the doctor found a very old photograph of a woman and a boy holding hands. The woman's fleshy body under her tight skirt, two plumpish arms, a fan clasped in her left hand—all of this is clearly visible in the picture. But the upper section of the photograph is blotchy, worn, making the woman's face unrecognizable. Could she be Angiolina, the alleged heartthrob of the watchman in his adolescence? Our archives confirm that "the divine Milanese soprano," as she was proclaimed by the citizenry, did in fact make a visit to Manaus on a December night in the year 1910.

Another hypothesis, suggested by Dr. S.L., proposes that the woman in the photograph is a local Amazonian pianist known to have given several recitals during the time Seu Álvaro worked as a watchman at the Opera House. Who could forget the story of how she later drowned not far from the "Meeting of the Waters"? Her last concert, *Sunrise Sonata in F Minor,* also looms large in the memory of the whole city, though no doubt recalled with greatest intensity by that boy, now so ancient.

Senhor de Mato's psychological condition remains undiagnosed. Will he turn out to be merely a mythomaniac? Simply suffering from somniloquy? A victim of a crisis of delirium tremens? What he saw, or said he saw—will it prove to have been lunatic delusions? A resident of the Praça São Sebastião swears that she saw a pregnant woman dragging herself into the Opera House. Yesterday's thunderous downpour didn't cause her to veer from her course for a minute, said our informant, who, we should point out, is a regular reader of this weekly column, Truth Is a Seven-Headed Beast.

Translated by Ellen Doré Watson

The Last Tango in Jacobina

Márcia Denser

IT WAS LIKE ONE OF THOSE THINGS that's hard to explain, you can only feel it seething, throbbing, and repelling—because it does repel—and, because of all that, you just know it's going to end up badly. It would be as impossible to avoid it as to suffer its aftermath which was evident, in a sense, in its origin, its meaning.

The paulistana writer MÁRCIA DENSER is best known for her work in fiction and journalism. Her major literary publications include *O Animal dos motéis* (1981), *Exercícios para o Pecado* (1984), *Diana Caçadora* (1986), *Histórias* (1986), *Toda Prosa* (2002), and the recent novel *Caim: Sagrados laços frouxos* (2006). She has edited many anthologies, including two volumes of erotic fiction which contain short stories by some of Brazil's most notable women writers. Denser's work has been translated into English, German, Dutch, and Russian. This story, which appeared in 1985 in *Histórias de amor infeliz (Stories of Unhappy Love)*, is evocative of the strained nature of love relationships in Denser's earlier work and exemplifies some of her best writing to date.

I'm talking about my passion for Mingo, something so much a part of the red Porsche that this double inheritance seemed perfectly natural from the old man who, in reality, thought he was only leaving me the car, never perceiving Mingo as anything more than a mere accessory of the Porsche. A sophisticated guy is always a bit distracted and this doesn't mean that the old man was too proud or even a jerk; besides, I would have preferred to see him as someone who was at a higher plane (because that way, even at a lower level, at least I would exist), rather than knowing he was somewhere else, that is, nowhere at all.

So, falling in love with Mingo was like besmirching the memory of the old man. Literally. So much sweat, so much grease, and that murky passion. It was like I myself killing him a second time, by means of a pain that could no longer reach him, but killing him, at any rate, to get back at him for having abandoned me so soon, so alive, so alone, and afraid of so many things, precisely because Mingo was nothing but a mechanic, from the town of Jacobina in Bahia—I discovered that he was from Jacobina when he showed me his I. D. there in the bakery: a yellowish photo scarcely showing his vague, dim outline—the aureola of the ghost of a migrant boy's face out of which only his eyes bulged like two pointed pinheads, aggressive, shining with fear, and the rest of him floated adrift on a blazing road during the drought of '67, because that's where he came from at age 15.

But I'll say one thing for sure: he was an honest guy, so full of purity, honor, and dignity that it just wouldn't be right to scorn him, spit on him, invent antidotes to kill the pain, and to tell him all this now, even if he could

hear me, wouldn't help at all, it would sound so fucking cynical, all this shit that they always vomit on the
caskets at funerals, when we'd be capable of praising the
devil himself simply because we're alive and he's dead, so
it wouldn't help at all, the one who's dirty inside is me and
I can't even blame the old man for having loved only two
things at the end of his life: me and the Porsche.

Because my mother doesn't count.

It's been a long time since she ceased to exist, crys-
tallized in that dimension whose time and space, days
and nights, revolve around the twilight zone of the hairdresser, the masseuse, afternoon teas and the boutiques,
all within the neighborhood geography of the Jardins,
and the fashion shows that, Lord knows how, are indis-
tinguishable from the seasons, but that help to pass the
time.

I remember her at home, almost always sprawled out
on a red velvet sofa, her sigh, quickly swallowed up by
the inscrutable expression of a bored she-wolf, calm and
motionless like the surface of a swamp, or that monotonous, unmodulating voice that prattled on and on, the
sudden swishing of a negligee disappearing through a
door, dragging the interminable telephone cord (because
the conversations with her friends are also interminable
and always the same, labyrinthine), a sort of Ariadne's
thread that gradually winds around Chinese vases,
statuettes, antique chests, bronze pedestals, Chippendale
tables, disappearing under the drapes, under the heavy,
perpetually closed curtains that filter a fine mist of hys-
terical particles, creating that gritty atmosphere of red
and hot ashes of Pharaonic tombs, while she weaves and

unweaves the same mindless yarn, endlessly returning to the sofa, to sighing, and to boredom.

Through her obsession with preserving her youth and stopping time, she ended up mummifying herself. She and her withered camellias, her purple taffeta dresses, her trinkets buried at the bottom of the closet full of mirrors, in the depth of mirrors.

When I remember Mingo, what comes back to me is the circular recollection of those dirty, greasy fingernails extended in a last, useless attempt to reach me through the windshield, that stunned, bewildered look, that half-opened mouth, eternally suspended in the question that will never have an answer.

He's not the one who's stalking me though—it's my ghosts. But my psychiatrist says, It's the same thing, Julia, and my mother: When are you going to grow up, Julia? And I can only imagine what it is to be an adult because the fact that I'm 24 and have a little experience in life—I mean with the carousing and all—it seems that none of this means anything or changes a thing because all this bingeing is part of a same, single, continual, permanent fling, the routine of one who lives chasing emotions and forbidden adventures for the sake of mere existential experimentalism, what I've put in place of deception, and practice with a certain distracted virtuosity, exactly like the old man (because I inherited all this, not by chance but by bitter destiny and by coincidence, from that adorable old man, my father), as if life occurred in a dream or in a film and, I, made of flesh and blood, at the end, as the curtain falls, as the day dawns, as if I really had nothing to do with all this.

There's also the thing about the drinking sprees—my mother says I'm just like the old man in that way too, but my psychiatrist doesn't agree, he says the old man was the old man and I am me, on that much we agree—but I need to stop, without any doubt; the time will come, I know, when I'll have to stop, I just don't know how or when, it's sort of like a compulsion: we keep getting happier between the end of the second and the first half of the third bottle of wine, unashamedly happy and free of worries and anxieties about the future and about the fears and ghosts I've already mentioned, and, besides, two or three bottles can't do any harm, right? No. Wrong. Because I don't stop at the second or third; I don't stop until I black out, that's it—that's what turns me on to so much insanity, like with Mingo, I imagine myself a courtesan, like a Du Barry or Pompadour, a milady, from Dumas' novels: a libertine, suave, cruel, generous, envied, mysterious, desired, hated, always unobtainable. I could never imagine myself a queen—they're so open to attack, they can't operate behind the scenes, and after all, they're the ones who receive and pay History's bills—a queen abdicates personhood to be a queen whereas I, with my Spanish shawls, my curls à la Schneider, my red pants, Italian boots, honeysuckle perfume, so beautiful, so sexy, and so adorably drunk, yes, because I needed more than four shots (four good strong shots) to unleash what had been dragging on silently between Mingo and me ever since the first time I took the Porsche to the garage by myself, some two months after the old man's death, and there he was: shy, respectful, competent, avoiding my bold, spoiled-girl stare that disguised the wicked huntress who would drag a man down under so much grease, so much sweat and shame, looking down at the carburetor with a wrench in his hand, and what would he do if I, a courtesan from the novels . . . ?

But all that was before, before that Saturday in January.

Three years had already gone by since the old man had died and between the two of us, Mingo and me, an ambiguous relationship had been established between the capricious customer and the faithful employee who was resigned to the heel of authority and would drop what he was doing the minute the snout of the red Porsche appeared at the entrance to the garage, inevitably provoking the boss, an acerbic Spaniard who stank of garlic, whose repressed anger was noticeable in the deplorable, sallow hue that tinged his face, what the fuck, Mingo was his best mechanic, the source of good profit, who was paid a miserable salary. In reality, I, my money, and that damned imported car represented a real subversion of the order. But Mingo couldn't have cared less, because, without realizing it, he was obeying a more powerful force, perhaps the awakening of the ancient slave who, in a dazed stupor, offers the nape of his neck to the delicate foot of the little mistress, experiencing a nameless pleasure at being stepped on and humiliated, from time immemorial, that paradox towards which he throbbed and whined insidiously, because I too was a slave, a captive, it would have been my place to raise him up from the dust, give him my hand, drag him to the supreme transgression, given that catastrophes were always a feminine specialty, right? Those eternal children. "When are you going to grow up, Julia?" as if I could flee my serpentine fate.

That Saturday I got out of the taxi, I was coming home from a copiously alcoholic luncheon, stopped at the entrance to the garage and saw Mingo from behind, shining the fender of the Porsche with a rag, his pants and shirt so dirty that you couldn't tell what color they once were, if they ever even had any color, his gnarled, dark feet emerging like roots from two tin cans, similar to those small, rickety trees unworthy of the soft, moist soil, wild enough to suffocate in a vase, that grow, abandoned, in tin cans at the rear of the backyard where they adapt marvelously, sprouting right through the holes corroded by the rust, the wind, the rain, the hot sun, disowned, complacent, and stupefied, nobody ever bothering to throw them away. In a way, Mingo resembled those abstract paintings, furiously made up of so many layers of spots and smudges that it was nearly impossible to distinguish between what was paint, dust, oil, sweat, grease, rags, tears—that repulsive concoction of work—generating contradictory feelings in me that shifted violently between tenderness, pity, and desire—that repulsive concoction of passion—and there I was, standing there, when he turned around and looked at me with those clean, dark, Oriental eyes, the only clean thing on that sooty face, that color way beyond soiled, the color of someone who lives lower than the lowest, under cars, that skin upon which the sun alone had left its scourge, the delicate wrinkles in whose grooves ashes and dust were permanently ingrained, and my eyes ran down the thin, angular body, different from the resilient, healthy slenderness of the boys at the pool and the track, Mingo's rigid, taut scrawniness, as if the gears needed greasing, something that had started with manioc flour and brown sugar, evolving into rotgut booze and cheap meals from the corner bar, something that survived in spite of malnutrition, hence the primitive harshness, the retreat of a semi-domesticated animal, the awkwardness, the bad manners in the presence of ladies.

But I admired Mingo, wizard of the mysteries of the machine, the interpreter of its metal entrails, of the secret laws of that universe of cylinders and axles and bushings and bearings and *made in Germany from Jacobina?* But Mingo is special, Julia. Why, Daddy? I'm fixing a Firebird, Mr. Max. Don't melt your wings, Mingo. What wings, Mr. Max? A bird can only fly, Julia.

It was a hot, sunless Saturday, a sticky afternoon of sweat and steamy haze that promised to drown the city at night as in a black barrel of asphalt.

Mingo smiled: it's finished. Get in, I said, I want to see if it's up to snuff. He smiled again, as if to say do you doubt it? and agreed, a bit reluctantly, because it took him a few seconds to catch on and be surprised by the invitation, an invitation to go for a ride is quite different from going out with a customer to test the car, there was a dark, impenetrable undercurrent in my voice, maybe she's plastered, he must have thought, lied, trying to fool himself, still trying to get the grease off his fingers with a rag.

I pulled out, burning rubber. I love to show off. That really turned Mingo on. I can't even guess how long we rode around, I was in a zone outside of time that was frozen by an incessant, eternal, vertiginous racing up and down streets and around squares, roller-coasting one hill after another, whipping along the avenues, green, red, brake, accelerate, weaving in and out, the sun sinking over São Francisco Plaza and appearing again on an unexpected curve in the Aclimação district, and I thought the city could also be infinite, I who judged it only huge and unsuspecting, never thought of it as sudden and simultaneous, monotonous like the universe, infinitely agonizing, while talking about cars, Mingo's passion, which is to talk about all cars and only one car, me asking a slew of questions which he answered more and more distractedly, slowly, monosyllabically, like an animal quieting down, like someone who leans over a blank piece of paper on which somebody else will write a verdict or a message in indecipherable code, knowing ahead of time that he'll have to carry it out even though something inside him still resists, something he can't name because he can't think, because he's only a recoiling body. It's the bit, I thought, it can only be the bit those northeasterners have stuck in their mouth, that blind, stupid notion of honor, that permanent, retarded, mulish lack of self-confidence, the rigid laws of the barren backlands by which they have always lived and where, beyond those protective limits, lurk hunger, poverty, death, hence impossible to transcend, unthinkable to explore such strange feelings of madness and ambition because they're the children of the devil, prince of darkness in that world where all is evil and illusion, as his mother and his mother's mother used to say, in that torrid, squalid Jacobina.

But I wasn't interested in taking hold of that atavistic rein and making him change direction, going from one yoke to another wouldn't make any difference, he was already used to it; nor did I want to let loose of it once and for all: he'd come back even more submissive, begging for the whip, an abject creature without a trace of pride or dignity would do me no good; no, to have him the way I wanted him, I'd have to wear out the rein a little bit at a time and in different places, loosen it without him realizing it, corrupt him enough for him to serve me but not enough to free him, in short, intoxicate him with my seventy times seven times adulterated, vicious and vitiated Latin blood, retempered by two thousand years of arenas and aristocracy and that wasn't all, I'd have to see where I would take him, if I could take him anywhere, except to hell, my blind desire, my black horse, while it was getting dark and I waited in the car at the entrance to the garage for him to take a bath, put on a clean shirt, to buy him a beer. There was no hurry.

Seated on stools at the bar of the corner bakery, he ordered beers and a chaser which I tasted, making a face. He kept looking at me and chuckling, making fun of me, the shower, the clean clothes, men chattering in the background, the glaring lights, and the acrid smell of the kneading table which propelled him to his own surroundings, to what he was, Mingo, because perhaps he was wrong, but everything was the way it should be, as it always had been, even with Miss Julia, shooting the breeze, but there was still a bug in the carburetor, his guard completely down and then, yes, tilting my head, in a casual tone, like someone making a comment about the weather, I hit him with:

"You love me, don't you Domingos? Your name's Domingos, isn't it?"

"I what?" he gagged on the question.

"I want you too, you know?"

"I dunno about you, ma'am, but I sure do know about me," he murmured at last, turning his face away.

"Do you really?" I egged him on.

"I've liked you ever since that day when Mr. Max . . . sorry . . . it was so weird," he blurted out as he finished off his chaser.

"The old man? Are you talking about the old man? You can't forget him either, can you Mingo? I mean the way he was and all, a guy so . . . and then, snap, see me snap my fingers? Then the Great Son of a Bitch snapped his fingers and it was as if he never . . . as if he still . . . "

"Don't say that, Miss Julia, it's a sin. God's got his ways and we've gotta accept them. Forget all that. Don't cry no more. Take this hanky, ma'am, it's clean. Your make-up's gonna run."

"And stop calling me ma'am, what a pain!"

"OK, OK. You know, you're prettier when you cry?"

"I know, just like in the movies."

"What's this got to do with the movies? I'm just sayin' . . . "

"OK, I got excited. I forgot that you're not exactly a movie buff . . . "

"Who's got time? There's nights when I'm watchin' a western on TV and, bang, I'm out like a light. There's too many commercials . . . "

"I bet you're married. I don't see a ring but I'm sure you must be."

"You bet your life. I take it off because it gets greasy, that's the only reason. We've got three little kids. I'm buildin' a house . . . "

"Great. Where?" I asked just to ask, not too enthusiastically.

"Know Cangaiba?" and he laughed, "it's way the hell out there past Penha, you probably don't even know where it is, it's out in the boonies . . . "

"Even left of there," I interrupted, yawning.

"Yeah, out there," he agreed without understanding, "and so there's no money left over . . . "

And he shook his head, turning his shot glass with those long, dark, calloused fingers. Instinctively, I brushed them lightly. My hand was like a small, warm, soft, obscenely white bird perched on a knotty branch. He grabbed it, squeezed it tightly, convulsively, painfully, jealously, amazed by his boldness, amazed that he hadn't broken, smashed, pulverized it, feeling strange now with that contact, not because of its size or fragility, but because of something that, even if it had a name, couldn't be spoken.

"I want you," I whispered, and the words dripped onto the marble counter like a blasphemy spit by a devil into a holy water font, and they remained there, echoing, corroding.

Stunned, he raised his head, revealing two smashed blackberries where his eyes should have been, bloody spoils of the battle waged and lost. In a trembling voice, he recited the formula of surrender:

"With all due respect . . . may I?"

In silence, with my eyes half closed, I waited for his mouth to touch mine. There were a lot of people watching, but what difference does it make if we were consummating what was getting closer and closer anyway, the wet, brown shoreline of a beach where I would drown, lose myself in the deep murkiness and sargasso, infinitely abandoning myself to its warm poisonous undertow, to what was perhaps on the other side, a mermaid tied to the mast of an abandoned ship between reefs of pleading Ulysses, until the return of the kiss to the lonely mouth which now was nothing more than traces of booze and cigarettes, because once again life panted on my face; its foul breath of panic, shame, passion, and insult and of all that mixed together, not to mention the Portuguese bartender who never tired of cleaning the counter, who pierced me with his eyes like knives thrown at a wall, of course, if it were your daughter, but it just so happens that I'm not your daughter, not the daughter of a scabby ass like you, my father is dead and very dead, I thought, glancing at a group of guys who glared at us loudly, and then I smiled: that's it, I, a courtesan of flesh and blood, with my two millennia can afford the luxury of . . . I felt someone grab my arm.

"Hey, what're you looking at?"—Mingo, eyes closed, jaws clenched—"cut out the flirting around, you hear?"

I lowered my head, but only to hide another smile, this time a bitter one. And, on the other hand, that's it too, in other words, the same thing, and everything goes on as it should. Even the whore of Babylon. I struggled to get my fingers inside his hand that had locked silently, stubbornly like a jammed tool. Doggedly, I tried and tried, but it wouldn't budge. Furious, I began to look for my purse, grab my shawl, ready to leave him there in that filthy bar, when I was grabbed by an iron fist that immobilized my arm, squeezing it brutally until I moaned:

"Let go, you son of a bitch!"

"Your mother's the bitch!"

"And of the best kind! Let go!"

"That'll teach you not to fool around with a man. If you want something with me, it's gotta be my way."

I stopped struggling and confronted him with a defiant look that seemed somewhat ridiculous on a face so red with hatred, my jaw trembled with so much silly, helpless anger which he noticed and repaid with a look mixed with disdain, triumph, and condescending pity, taking advantage of my irritation to squeeze my arm again. Then slowly, almost imperceptibly, gently, and tenderly, I broke into a smile, a smile the meaning of which he would never guess in two thousand years because men just don't learn, that's all there is to it. He eased up on the squeeze and almost immediately there he was, whining sorry, sorry, groveling, please, humiliating himself, it's all over, love, give it up, love, it gets awfully tedious, OK, OK, love, and so on for more than fifteen minutes, the dirty ritual of reconciliation. So we made up.

He ordered two more beers and another chaser to celebrate.

"Hey," I remembered, "wanna go dancing?"

"Yeah, I'd like to but I dunno how," he answered, a smile shining in his eyes.

"I'll teach you. I know a place . . . "

"What place?"

"A night club . . . "

"Good girls don't hang out in night clubs."

"My father used to go there."

"Your father was a man."

"And what are you?"

"Me? I'm broke."

"Don't give me that."

"What do you mean don't gimme that?"

"Let's make a deal. How much was the bill for my car?"

"Nothing," he growled, staring hard at me.

"What do you mean, nothing?"—I turned my head—"fine, you don't want to go out with me . . ."

"Hold on a minute. I'll be right back."

He got up and left. I thought to myself: he's going to set up an IOU with the Spaniard. Spend what he doesn't have. Shitty, stupid pride. He came back:

"Let's go. It's all taken care of."

The place was called *Noches de Ronda*. My father used to go there at the end of his nights out, on certain, particularly bitter nights. A small, dingy night club that had never known its heyday, which means it survived thanks to its clientele made up of men with threadbare suits, young whores from the suburbs, police investigators, trashy bohemians: the very best of the city mongrels. Nonetheless, it had its painful, ironic poetry, the old man must have thought shortly before dying, raising his brows, his eyes half shut, a cigarette smoldering in the ashtray, already on the seventh or eighth drink, dawn breaking and the chauffeur outside shivering and stomping his feet and what the hell is that son of a bitch doing in there hanging around with a bunch of low-lifes.

Very dark, cluttered with little greasy stools and minuscule tables around which two or three ill-humored waiters hovered like bats in worn-out red jackets, in that purplish atmosphere saturated with smoke and lost illusions. On the worn-out dance floor beyond, a wretched band despondently played boleros and Paraguayan *guarânias*. The big attraction was old Cacho and his accordion. The owner Carlito was a pale Argentinean, a vaguely untrustworthy air in the soul of a fallen angel, eternally keeping track of the tabs, either out of forgetfulness or indifference (that silent, implicit fraternity that brings together and mixes those creatures of the night), perpetually wandering around in his cloud of gloom as if adrift in the forgotten pain that lurked in his permanently glazed eyes, lost in a sky of paper aluminum stars and 500 cc of dietilaminapropanilfenoma, liquid solution.

"Good evening!" he greeted, as he drew near. A nervous tic drew taut his right cheek spoiling the smile that oscillated between a grimace and a frown.

"It's a bit dead tonight," he said casually, as if apologizing. It was obvious that nothing mattered much to him, but, after all, one had to say something to the distinguished clientele.

"*Para usted,* the usual, *chica?* And for the gentleman?"

At that moment his indifferent glance focused on the strange figure at my side. Slightly arching his thick dark eyebrows, he gave me a questioning look. I winked.

"The same for the gentleman," I answered, pronouncing the word "gentleman" with unintentional irony.

Carlito smiled compassionately, *pobre chica,* another of her flings, he must have thought. He understood those things better than I did. Bowing, he took off in haste after the waiter.

Several couples undulated on the dance floor to the tune of something between *El Reloj* and *La Barca.* Over at the tables, the fleeting flame of a lighter, the embers of cigarettes, dramatically and momentarily revealed confused shapes sunken in darkness, fragments of a tense embrace behind glasses and bottles, pale, tired, or intense faces, fleeting mouths caught in a red sentence, the tail end of a stentorian laugh lost again in an indistinct murmur, hands caressing bleached hair, a thigh of shiny tropical wool draped over green satin thighs, red, purple, ruby-red claws, freckles, and wrinkles, and the glint of a wedding ring on a hairy hand, bodies entwining and separating, whispering, drunken, throbbing shadows, "*por que tu barca tiene que partir?*" on the lookout for what was lurking down below, "*hasta que tu decidas,*" after dancing, after leaving, drenched in so much sweat, booze and exhaustion.

The drinks arrived. Mingo embraced me and looked around skittishly, squeezing my shoulders with his cold, arched fingers entangled in the fringe of my shawl. He clung to me as if to protect himself from an unknown terror, that bewildering sensation of the unreal that assaults children and animals, kissing me like a madman or a castaway, poor Mingo, I thought, delicately pushing him away, drinking the watered-down whisky, sensing that something was gradually evaporating, dissipating, and my soul, afloat, was about to envelop old Cacho at the first chords of what was a very sad, very old tango, truncated moans of that tango mutilated by certain absent beats which my memory filled in with feeble, silent, consecutive explosions; the vague, feared, hazy, incomplete image of Max, of the old man, he who, in spite of myself, I once called father, relentlessly appearing and disappearing, fading out and coming into view and restoring in me that trembling recollection of sea-green eyes, a red carnation in his lapel, his hand extended to the lady in yellow who, in a stiff theatrical gesture, let herself be held like a doll. Clasped together, their bodies intersected with chronometric precision: a stop, two pirouettes, and on they went, tragically synchronized, duplicating parallel steps that flowed together into one syncopated figure, an elaborate geometry of skips, knees, thighs, that never touched for fear of missing the beat, shattering the rosette, because the tango is a labyrinth of music imprisoned within mordant walls of sighs where the same interminable choreography is always played out, a happy prisoner of symmetry and devoid of hope, while old Cacho, on this side of reality, went on playing, perhaps out of sheer reflex action and spasms, as if he had died minutes before the final notes which his accordion, loosely and uncontrollably, ground out blindly without old Cacho's soul there to breath more feeling into it.

Blinded by tears, I pulled Mingo onto the dance floor. He resisted, "I dunno how to dance to that." I insisted, "It doesn't matter, nobody knows how."

Between the couples, marionettes imitating a gross pantomime of a tango that could hardly be heard, of the tango that only I could hear, turning in front of Mingo, in front of that northeasterner who smelled of sweat and gasoline, the wet look of a dog, miserably grotesque and stiff as a stump, in front of the residue of that inferior race, of all those scraps thrown together by chance and cast into the world by some stupid devil, of that cruel slap of reality that expelled me from what was most mine and returned me to the present, that putrid parody of the past, ironically called *Noches de Ronda,* and, in supreme mockery, with a filthy mulatto in front of me.

Nauseated, I crossed the dance floor as if immersed in a mud puddle of glowing vapors, constantly running away from the shadow that haunted me, endlessly pursuing the one who was waiting for me outside, in the car, at the door of this bitter night: "Let's go, Julia/It's late, daddy/I'll let you drive, dear/Try it with a banana/Hum, that's not quite right, but we'll manage/Look, however/wherever, *pick-me-up, honey.* Haven't you read Fitzgerald?/*Tender is the Night*?/This kind of pea soup seen through the windshield is tender . . . We'd be better off inside the book/But we aren't/You're right, we aren't/OK I skipped some parts/It's a shame . . . /That part that says . . . /Oh, well, you know how sensitive the Americans are about names/It doesn't make sense/So, I'll explain. Page 257, here it is: *Pick-me-up,* it's something like "take me with you. A drink . . . "

I got in the car and started it. I heard the engine roar and roar and then the crushing, metallic smash. I floored the accelerator furiously, not even noticing the car wasn't moving. Then I looked up and saw the man illuminated by the headlights: eyes bulging, mouth twisted, a black tuft of kinky hair, arms open over the hood, a red pulp between my red Porsche and the slender, black shadow of the post. As if he had fallen from a cross. Then the insanity of shouts, lights, sirens, and anonymous hands grabbing, pushing and tearing at me pitilessly, hot, sweet liquid running down my face, traces of sweat, booze, and dried up grease in the depths of my conscience, and then the night blacked out. Pitch-black. Extinguished, for a time without an answer, I can no longer remember how long I've been waiting between clean sheets and merciful hypodermic needles for that perpetual, pale dawn that doesn't break, doesn't dawn, doesn't forget.

Translated by Peggy Sharpe

The Miracle of the Birds

Jorge Amado

THE MIRACLE OCCURRED on a lively market day in Piranhas, a town on the São Francisco River in the state of Alagoas, Brazil. It was witnessed by hundreds of townspeople, running the social gamut from a rich colonel named Jarde Ramalho, who had seen action against Lampião, the Bandit of the Backlands, to dirt farmers in

JORGE AMADO (1912-2001) is Brazil's best-known 20th-century novelist. Translated into fifty languages, highly praised by both Camus and Sartre, winner of the 1951 Stalin Peace Prize, he is one of the few Brazilian literary figures with an international reputation. His vision encompasses every level of society and all races, focusing sympathetically on the lower classes of his beloved Bahia. Following his early days as a social-protest writer (*The Violent Land*, *The Golden Harvest*), he became a skillful portrayer of the picturesque (and picaresque) Brazilian Northeast in highly acclaimed works like *Gabriela, Clove and Cinnamon*, *Dona Flor and Her Two Husbands* (later a successful film), and *Tent of Miracles*. Also available in English are *Sea of Death*, *Tieta*, *Home is the Sailor*, and *Showdown*. "The Miracle of the Birds," which he called a fable, was his last published work.

town for the day to sell their manioc flour and fresh-picked corn. An illustrious visitor who was being feted that day in Piranhas, the widow of our great regional novelist Graciliano Ramos, saw it too; and since Dona Heloísa Ramos is notoriously truthful, her testimony alone should be enough to prove the veracity of my tale.

The protagonist in this affair was Ubaldo Capadócio, known far and wide for his competence in the three trades of lover, minstrel, and composer of popular ballads, which were printed up in leaflets and pinned to a clothesline, to be sold in the marketplace. His antagonist was Captain Lindolfo Ezequiel, whose reputation for primitive courage and cruelty was a byword in the state of Alagoas, where men are undeniably men. Exactly what kind of captain he was is unclear, but everyone knew he had earned his stripes by dispatching other men to the graveyard. The two occupations for which he was famous were those of hired killer, which paid well and earned him respect, and husband to Sabô—a position requiring uncommon ability, energy, and constant violent threats to the masculine population. For Sabô, if truth be told, respected neither her husband's military rank nor his ugly scowl and the lethal weapon he wore. Sabô flaunted herself in front of all the men and figured in the dreams of every last one of them (including boys under fourteen) whether single, married, engaged, or living with another woman. But the only person brave enough to risk arousing the captain's murderous masculine pride and an unceremonious death from the barrel of a gun was Sabô herself. All the men who were hot for her ground their teeth, tucked their tails between their legs, and turned their eyes away from Sabô the siren.

All but Ubaldo Capadócio. Not because he was reckless or brave as a lion, but out of sheer ignorance of local
custom. After all, he was only a stranger passing through
in search of readers and a bustling marketplace where
he could sell the ballads he had composed (the latest of
which, "The Story of the Society Lady Who Fell in Love
with a Werewolf," was selling like hotcakes, and deserved
to); a party where he could play his concertina and impro-
vise verses; and an inviting bed where he could rest from
his labors and snuggle up to a pretty brunette. Whatever
his motive, the fact is that he did brave the bully, and
what's more he did it in a woman's shortie nightgown; the
top of Sabô's pink baby-doll pajamas, to be exact.

Ubaldo Capadócio the minstrel was a heartbreaker
and a fine figure of a man: tall, lean, and nimble, with
a tousled mop of hair and an easy laugh. A gifted con-
versationalist in any company, he knew how to season
his talk with wit and learning; wherever he found himself, an animated circle formed instantly around him.
All through the vast back country of Bahia and Sergipe
where he worked, worried, and loved, Ubaldo was loved
in return and his talents were always in demand. He was
showered with invitations to enliven christenings, wed-
dings, and wakes; he had no equal when it came to toast-
ing a bride and bridegroom, or telling stories at a wake
that could make a dead man laugh or cry. And that's no
idle expression. It really happened and I could round up
plenty of live witnesses to prove it. I'll mention just two
of them here: master artist Calasans Neto and Florisvaldo
Matos, the troubadour of Sergipe. They both saw the
deceased Aristóbulo Negritude burst out in a horse laugh,

right where he lay dead as a doornail in his coffin, when Ubaldo Capadócio told the story of the beached whale in Maragogipe. I won't ask my friend Carybe the painter to testify because everybody knows he's a liar. The way he tells it, Negritude didn't just laugh, he added a dirty twist to the story as well. But those of us in the know say it was Carybe—no upstanding citizen—who put in the smutty details himself. Aristóbulo may have been a know-it-all but he drew the line at butting in on another man's story; he knew how a proper corpse ought to behave.

It was at shindigs that Ubaldo really shone. Concertina clasped to his breast, husky voice soaked in rum, languorous imploring eyes, fingers sliding sensuously over the keys, with his playing he charmed sighs and promises from young girls, married women, kept women, fallen women, disconsolate widows (consoling widows came naturally to a generous nature like Ubaldo's). Along with the deep sighs and ardent promises there was usually a barrage of threats and curses, but Ubaldo was no coward and just plowed right ahead.

Wanderer though he was, he had a house and home— several houses and homes—in Bahia and Sergipe. Why not, with his good looks and his reputation? So many women and Ubaldo was true to all of them, for his was a faithful, constant heart. He never broke off with a woman (except for Braulia, but Braulia, for heaven's sake . . .), never sent one away. They left of their own accord, loudly claiming they had been used and betrayed, when they found out about all the others, though how abstinence could be expected of a romantic wandering bard away from home for weeks and months at a time I don't know.

These abrupt partings were never Capadócio's idea and they always made him unhappy. Whenever a woman left him he felt as if he were losing the only one in the world. However many others there might be, each one was the only one, and if that riddle baffles you then you don't know much about love. What could be the cause of such repeated ingratitude, such unreasoning selfishness, when he, Ubaldo Capadócio, could always be counted on as a breadwinner, a prop, and a mainstay to his women, with more than enough skill and imagination to satisfy them all and to spare?

Some women, in fact, didn't abandon him but took him the way he was. Which explains why, at the time of the miracle in Piranhas, Ubaldo Capadócio, at thirty-two years of age, was maintaining three families on his earnings as a popular poet, balladeer, and musician. What with his concertina and his guitar, his husky voice and his rhymes—rich rhymes or poor, it didn't matter—it was poetry that put food on the table for his three wives, none of them lawfully wedded, and nine children, three of whom were not his.

Two of the households were traditionally constituted families complete with wife and children, while the third had not yet produced any offspring. For Rosecler, the new addition, who was still in the honeymoon stage, it was too early for pregnancy and birth; Ubaldo spent more on the rings, bracelets, necklaces, and other baubles she loved than on either of the other two; in return Rosecler gave him passionate tenderness, a mixture of honey and pepper.

Ubaldo Capadócio, then, was running over with rhymes and with children, only half a dozen of whom, as we've said, were his by blood: three with Romilda, three with Valdelice. Of the three adopted boys, the eldest came with Romilda when this handsome mulatto woman decided to leave her husband behind his counter in Aracaju and follow the plangent chords of the lonely troubadour's guitar. Yes, lonely and forlorn, because when a man wants a certain woman—when he's so hungry for her he can't get her out of his mind—even if he's playing around with other women day and night he might as well be alone; that one confounded woman is the only companion who can cheer him up and cure him of his lonesome blues. Seeing him brought so low, Romilda softened and bundled up her things, but first she told him she was willing to leave her husband but not her little boy; that she couldn't be separated from him. "He'll be my son," swore Capadócio dramatically with his hand on his heart. He didn't care whether she brought along one child, three children, or four; it was all the same to him, he was so crazy to get Romilda into bed, touch her breasts, stroke her thighs. "Bring your little boy, bring your nephew, bring your whole family if you want to!"

The second boy, named Dante after the poet, was adopted by Capadócio and Valdelice after his mother died, leaving the six-month-old baby with a fierce case of dysentery. Entrusting him to his father was out of the question. Bernardo Sabença, a talented storyteller and improviser who could drink his bar companions under the table, had no aptitude whatever for child-rearing, especially when the child had loose bowels and stank.

As for the third boy, nicknamed Cavy because he shared that rodent's voracious appetite, they knew nothing at all about his parents, age, name, but had simply picked him up by the side of a back-country road eating clay, which isn't nourishing but tastes pretty good. After a close examination of Cavy's features and ways—fair hair, blue eyes, clever hands that were quick to grasp any object within reach—Valdelice, who was something of an amateur psychologist, concluded that his father must have been a lordly landowner, a "doctor," and that he had inherited his dark complexion from his mother.

For those who want more precise information about Capadócio's family life, I'll just add that he sometimes resided with the fair Romilda in Lagarto in the state of Sergipe, while the Valdelice-Capadócio residence was in Baraúnas Alley, Amargosa, Bahia. Love-hungry young Rosecler lives in Bahia too, in a suburb of a big city, Jequiê. Ubaldo Capadócio kissed his three wives with a cheery "So long, see you soon" (no one but a dead man on the way to his funeral ought to say the word "goodbye") and set off to make his fortune in the famous state of Alagoas, where life is cheap but poetry is prized; where a talented minstrel can reap applause, earn good money, and, if he's brave enough, warm the bed of some fine brunettes.

Ubaldo's expedition into the rugged Alagoan backlands was going splendidly. At parties, fairs, christenings, even a bishop's pastoral mission to Arapiraca, Ubaldo Capadócio turned up with his concertina, his guitar, and a suitcase full of ballads all ready to hang on the line, raking in a fair harvest of coins and breaking hearts right and left. After some time he reached the São Francisco River and made his way along its banks until he came to Piranhas. The scene of our story was famous for the beauty of its setting, for its colonial houses, and for having stood fast against Lampião's band years ago, a feat sung in many a ballad of the time. Yet another source of local pride was the fact that the town sheltered within its unbreached stone walls the aforementioned Captain Lindolfo Ezequiel and his legal wife, Sabô, also aforementioned but clearly deserving more ample reference to her graceful form, her dancing walk, a rear end that was a living legend, the dimples in her cheeks, and the way the hussy bit her lips to make them redder, as if saying, Oh yes, I'd like to, ooh, I wish I could, and so on and so forth. Sabô wasn't a woman at all; she was a temptation of the devil turned loose in Piranhas. But what man was reckless enough to give in? Yes, Piranhas was the home of the brave, the dauntless, the bold—Lampião could have borne witness to that. On the other hand, Lindolfo Ezequiel had already dispatched a fair number of his neighbors to the other world, some at the behest of powerful men, in order to make good money for himself and his free-spending wife, and others on his own hook because he mistrusted their intentions toward the virtuous Sabô. In the mind of her just but jealous husband, Sabô was a snow-white dove.

Our troubadour, Ubaldo Capadócio, had been in trouble over women more than once. He had jumped out of windows, jumped over fences, jumped over walls, streaked through the bushes, burst into other people's houses yelling for help, and plunged headlong into the Paraguassu River. One time a bullet had dusted his jacket but Xango, his powerful spirit guide, protected him. Actually, since the would-be avenger was a military man and a sharpshooter, Ubaldo was never in much danger of being hit.

As soon as he got to Piranhas he made for Sabô's bed, which also belonged, by right of lawful marriage lines from priest and judge, to Lindolfo Ezequiel. The captain and his artillery happened to be off on a short business trip to a distant town, where a congressman had a little job for him to do.

"Coast is clear," poor little Sabô called softly, so anxious to make the most of her chance.

Not that Ubaldo hadn't been given fair warning from a fellow versifier, the owner of the pension where he was staying: "Better stay clear, pal, Lindolfo has more than thirty notches on his gun, not counting the first few before he started hiring himself out as a professional."

Ubaldo didn't put much stock in what he heard; he knew what braggarts Alagoans are, and besides, to him women were always worth taking risks for.

He crossed Sabô's threshold at nightfall and was seen. He was still there the next morning when the sun was high in the sky; the affectionate girl couldn't get enough of him, and as for the balladeer, when he found a partner worthy of his mettle he liked to show off, not just his fire and potency, but all of his refinements and skill. He was no ignoramus when it came to sex; he had frequented five-star establishments, including one where the madam was French, and had learned everything they had to teach. Ubaldo was one hell of a lover.

No one ever knew why Lindolfo Ezequiel doubled back on his tracks and got back to Piranhas when the weekly market was at its height, just when Ubaldo and Sabô were acting out the fast, fond, quintessential farewell, knowing time was getting short but drawing it out because they were weary, lingering tenderly because they already missed each other. And here came the killer waving his blunderbuss, puffing and threatening death preceded by castration in the public square. A curious crowd gathered behind him, the biggest since the Holy Week procession.

When Lindolfo set foot in the doorway Sabô recognized his tread. "That's my husband," she said with a giggle.

Ubaldo reacted instantly, as he always did on these occasions, and glanced swiftly around for something to cover his nakedness. He was no exhibitionist; in public he preferred to be decently dressed. All he could find in his haste was the top half of Sabô's pink baby-doll nightie, which he pulled on over his head. He was so tall the dainty garment didn't even reach his navel. But naked, as slandering tongues have it, he was not. He leaped through the window as the cuckold burst into the room, brandishing his revolver. Sabô, the chaste wife and innocent victim, accused the balladeer of trying to seduce her and rape her. But she had resisted heroically, and now she clamored for vengeance. "Don't worry, baby, I'm gonna tear his balls out and then shoot him in the head. Don't worry none about your reputation."

The two men pounded through the marketplace, the fleeing minstrel in his shortie nightgown, prick in full view and doomed balls swinging like the clapper of a bell. Hot on his heels and armed to the teeth came the captain with a wicked, sharp pig-gelding knife in his hand. Following close behind them was the eager crowd. Worn out from a night of celebration and a morning spent saying goodbye, Ubaldo Capadócio was losing ground. The killer and his knife were gaining on him and he felt a mortal chill in his balls.

Squarely in the middle of their path was the bird market, a whole pile of wooden cages stacked on top of one other, blocking the way. What with his speed and his fear Ubaldo couldn't veer around them fast enough. He crashed right into the wall of cages, and the birds, hundreds of them, fluttered free. One minute the air was full of birds—pigeons and thrushes, orioles and cardinals, canaries and lovebirds—and the next they had picked up Ubaldo Capadócio by his flimsy nightgown and flown away with him. Ahead of them, twelve macaws opened a pathway through the clouds, escorting the troubadour as lightly as a verse wafted by a zephyr.

Lindolfo Ezequiel was rooted to the spot in the middle of the square, where he remains to this day. He turned into a magnificent horntree, the biggest horntree in the Northeast, a unique source of raw material out of which artisans fashion combs, rings, drinking cups, and all kinds of other things. Thus the former killer was transformed into an object of real public utility. As for Sabô, she belongs to the whole community now, under the immediate protection of Colonel Jarde Ramalho, who attentively observed both the chase and the miracle.

The birds flew over Alagoas bearing Ubaldo Capadócio, his balls safely intact, on the breeze. When they had crossed the Sergipe state line they set him down in a convent, where the nuns welcomed him courteously and asked him no questions.

Translated by Barbara Shelby Merello

Carnival Traumas

João Ubaldo Ribeiro

I HAVE A FRIEND who says that all our problems come from childhood traumas. I'm inclined to believe she's right, because my problems with Carnival can only have been caused by the trauma I suffered at my first childhood dance, when I was living in Aracaju. I was dressed as Pierrot: blue silk outfit, pink tassels instead of buttons, a conical hat with another tassel on top, two circles of rouge on

---

JOÃO UBALDO RIBEIRO was born in 1941 on the island of Itaparica, in Bahia. One of his country's most celebrated contemporary authors, he has been a law professor, scriptwriter, and a journalist. Master of the novel, the short story, and the *crônica*, a reflection on day-to-day modern life, he won the Camões Prize, the highest honor for a Portuguese-language writer. His novels *An Invincible Memory*, *Sergeant Getúlio*, and *The Lizard's Smile* have appeared in English translation, and *The House of the Fortunate Buddhas* is forthcoming. Since 1994, Ribeiro has been a member of the Brazilian Academy of Letters, the forty-member group known as "the immortals." "Carnival Traumas" is a humorous look at *Carnaval*, an institution deeply rooted in Brazilian tradition.

---

my face, lipstick, and powder. I came to suspect that my
mother would have preferred I'd been born a girl and that
if she could she'd have outfitted me as Colombina. The fact
is that I didn't want to go to the dance, and for the rest of
my life I've been a unique kind of carnival-lover, because I
favor Carnival in theory and oppose it in practice.

Not to mention, besides, that I suffered various other
traumas, some of which during adolescence or even afterwards as an adult, reinforced my feeling of abnormality
for not taking part in the revelry. I did everything to join
in, but to no avail. As a teenager, for example, I worked
up a trick with a friend who suffered from the same infir-
mity, a companion in misfortune both carnival-wise and
women-wise. In those days, when a guy went stag to a
dance, he would enter the ballroom and start jumping
around, sometimes with a small towel around his neck
to sniff ether. Suddenly he would spot a girl who was also
by herself, extend his arms forward and upward in her
direction, and the girl would come and dance with him.

A piece of cake, the two of us decided, after a couple
of hours observing the panorama of the party. It worked
with everyone. I didn't have the towel, but lots of guys
without towels were getting the girls, so we couldn't claim
to be missing any essential equipment. We watched the
maneuvers of several girl-getters and came to the conclusion that the technique wasn't a mystery. Arms extended,
a smile on your lips, jumping up and down to the rhythm
of the music, a confident air—and the girl was in the bag.
And so, after circling the room making an effort to feign
familiarity with and even indifference to the general pandemonium, we decided to enter the fray.

Ah, my friends, calling it adolescent trauma is putting it mildly. From my lookout spot at the edge of the ballroom I could see several girls who looked passable, despite the best ones being already taken, who should have been easy prey for revelers on the prowl. I had to be realistic, and I chose a bucktoothed girl wearing glasses. Quite possibly she was traumatized too and would welcome the solidarity of my outstretched arms. I took a deep breath, paced back and forth for a few minutes, and finally plunged into the midst of the ballroom. She was on the other side, which gave me time to stop feeling ridiculous jumping up and down with a smile that, I now realize, must have seemed carved out with a knife. I didn't back down, I went ahead with determination and courage. Finally, at a distance of six feet, I was face to face with the bucktoothed girl, raised my arms, and expected to have my hand on her shoulder in a few moments. But as soon as she saw me in that combat pose, she shot me a look that even today I dislike remembering, and did a devastating about-face. Sure, no one else noticed a thing, but I was permanently demoralized, a state reinforced by several other girls, and I gave up. Even today I don't extend my arms toward anybody; there's a limit to rejection, even after the age of sixty.

But the worst trauma was something I think I've already written about, some time ago. A lot of people, though, didn't have a chance to read it or don't remember, so I think I can retell the story. It was when, after several other tries, street carnivals and percussion bands, I gave in to pressure and decided to go out in Itaparica with a male cousin of mine, both of us in drag. My desire to be a carnival reveler was so strong that I thought if things worked out for me that way, I could join some transvestite group or other—fate is fate. So we got ready, each of us putting on one of those cloth masks with a red nose that used to be worn a lot in the past.

I must confess that, shortly after prancing around the island a bit, jumping here and there like that, I found it not to be that much fun. Neither did my cousin, but since he was a practical-minded and enterprising young man, he decided that, if we weren't enjoying ourselves, we could at least get something out of the situation. And of course what immediately came to mind was to rake in a few tips, a very common practice for the island's masked revelers in those days. And our target was a sure thing: my cousin's grandfather (and my great-uncle), who was rich, despite his not having a reputation for generosity— or maybe because of it. In any case, our ambition was limited to scoring a bit of change to at least compensate in part for our sacrifice in maintaining national tradition, without making a major dent in his fortune.

We arrived at his house, went in speaking in the falsetto used in the old days, and kidded around with everyone there, until we came to the old man. It was time to tease him and then ask for some small change. We went over to him, blithering foolishness that I can't remember, until he winked a lascivious eye at me and, before I could react, stuck his hand under my skirt. I jumped back like a shot.

"What're you doing, grampa? It's me!" I exclaimed, pulling off the mask.

"Heh heh heh," he said, without a scintilla of contrition. "If you don't wanna be one, don't dress like one!"

And even after everything was cleared up, he refused to give us a thing, claiming he didn't have a penny on him. Carnival—a disappointment.

Translated by Clifford Landers

The Pageant

by Flávio Carneiro

IT WAS THE TIME I LIKED THE MOST, definitely. Three in the afternoon, sheets whitening on the clothesline, the sun blazing on the flagstones of the porch, the four of us in the back yard, having fled the house with a colorful bundle of clothes under our arms: a carmine silk dress, a lacy pink skirt, our dead father's dark suit coat, a

FLÁVIO CARNEIRO was born in Goiânia in 1962, moved to Rio de Janeiro in the early 1980s, and has lived in Teresópolis since 2003. Novelist, scriptwriter, literary critic, and university lecturer, he has written twelve books and two screenplays, and teaches Brazilian and Comparative Literature at Universidade Federal do Rio de Janeiro. His fiction includes novellas for children and young people, a collection of short stories, and two novels. He has won many literary awards, most recently the Prêmio Barco a Vapor in 2007 for *A distância das coisas* (*The Distance of Things*). The film *Bodas de Papel* (*Paper Wedding*), which he co-wrote with Adriana Lisboa and André Sturm, won the Jury's Prize at the Pernambuco Film Festival in 2008. This story is in the anthology *Valores para Viver* (*Values to Live By*) and is a fine example of Carneiro's engaging, lyrical, and poetic style.

light-blue satin blouse that mommy had been given as a
present and had never worn, poor thing. Maria, so fair,
carried a parasol. And sometimes the necklace of fake
pearls (so fancy!) and the patent leather shoes that would
one day be mine but not yet, mommy used to say, and
daddy's favorite belts, now black and brown stripes on the
wall in the corner behind the wardrobe, after what happened, stored, stolen.

Maria, always first, my little sister, boldly clambering
up the rocks, steadying herself atop the wall, and walking
in that baby-sister way of hers with her parasol of bright
flowers on a yellow background, high heels, red lipstick,
rouge, patting her chestnut curls, wanting to be prettier
than mommy. Maria holding her head high, willowy,
trying to be thin, ever so poised, until she bumped into
the branch of the guava tree, which no one ever pruned,
and tumbled almost into Rita's arms. Rita, the oldest and
most suntanned, always laughing, even at daddy, the only
one, scooping Maria up as if she were her own daughter
and planting kisses on her weeping until they were both
rolling across the yard dirtying satin, shoes, suit coat,
mixing dust, leaves, the two of them laughing at branches
and tumbles, and finally hugging one another, exhausted,
on the ground, bellies up, mouths open to the sky, like
always, mommy used to say, the two loonies.

Then Clarice, the oh-so pretty one, more than mommy
I thought but never said it. Light, her delicate little feet
bare, wearing just a large white shirt of daddy's, the
sleeves rolled up to her elbows, Clarice pulling back her
long, straight black hair, fastening it at the back of her
neck, smiling at the three of us down below and looking,

being, definitely prettier than mommy but no one ever said anything, not even daddy. Clarice, the only olive-skinned one, colored by the sun and some plants I think, her skin tanned but not red like Rita's, so like the Indian woman on the wall in our room hypnotizing my sleepless nights, dreaming I was her, the Indian woman, and Clarice, her color contrasting with the white of the shirt and the teeth that she revealed and hid in such a bewitching smile that it even seemed on purpose.

Clarice motioning to me, for me to get up there with her, not afterwards, like normally, but together this time. The rocks, the wall, and suddenly me in a crimson dress, navy blue suede shoes, a silver clasp in my hair, seeing my sister there next to me, with me, gazing at me pretty, so like the afternoon.

I felt a lump growing in my throat, this thing, wanting to be said, and I realized I urgently needed something wondrous, from me, slowly leaving my mouth as if I didn't want it to come out like that, in the form of a word. But it did: Clarice, you are . . . splendid!

First, silence, centuries-long. Then applause. The three of them clapping, Rita and Maria below, Clarice next to me, my three sisters making me the winner of that afternoon, for the first time in my life, before I'd even begun my parade, always the weakest, poor thing. And then this: there I was, a statue, hearing clap clap clap, and Maria and Rita's laughter laced with dust, sunshine, and ·leaves, and my sister Clarice, with her enchanted gaze, splendid.

Translated by Alison Entrekin

Rituals

Adélia Prado

MY FATHER USED TO TELL THE STORY of one of his self-defined marks of refinement (another being the fact that he ate properly, with knife and fork).

"It was before I met your mother, during my first days in Paracatu, when I came back from the night shift black with grease. My sister Figeninha had made up a bed for

ADÉLIA PRADO is one of the foremost poets of Brazil, praised both in literary circles and in the mainstream media. *Veja* (Brazil's *Newsweek*) has called her "a writer of rare brilliance and invincible simplicity." Prado has also published six volumes of lyric narratives, including *Filandras* (2001) from which these two pieces are drawn. While place and landscape are more implicit than explicit in Prado's work, nearly everything she writes is set in her native city of Divinópolis (the place names in "Rituals" are neighborhoods), in the landlocked state of Minas Gerais, which has produced more poets and presidents than any other in Brazil. The characters in these pieces are typically Mineiro—reserved, religious, melancholy, silent, and judicious. A selection of Prado's poetry in English can be found in *The Alphabet in the Park*.

me with clean, fresh-smelling sheets, but I didn't have the heart to lie down in it. I fixed myself a place to sleep on the floor, it didn't matter how much she protested. I lived with her there for a whole year, and only Saturday and Sunday would I allow myself the luxury of sleeping in a bed."

Papa was Aunt Efigeninha's brother and godfather of Benedito, a cousin my age. We used to visit their house up near the river in Bom Pastor, the neighborhood where I myself longed to live. The kitchen was a few steps down from the rest of the house and had a contraption which, as a little girl, I assumed all railway men set up for their wives, a shelf made of wire screening, hung outside the window over the sink, so that dishes could drain onto the garden below. If a house didn't have one, I didn't like it, and decided straight off that the owner was insensitive. Maybe it was that improvised wire shelf that gave me the idea that I should marry a boy who worked for the railroad, and so be guaranteed stability and comfort. Never mind that my own father never made a shelf like that for our house, I was sure it was a necessity, and that every woman demanded one. It had to be my mother's fault that our house wasn't as nice as Aunt Efigeninha's, though I never would have traded my mother—complicated, difficult, always sighing, but so pretty!—for anyone. That's exactly what the world was like—fabulous and imperfect. I tried to imagine what it would be like to have it all: a house in Bom Pastor, with a wire shelf to drain the dishes, a boy cousin to play with, and no one finding fault.

When Benedito's family came to visit, he'd say, "Want to play 'Pass the Ring'?"

And it was so good I couldn't understand why no one stopped us! We were also allowed to play hide-and-seek. When Benedito found me, he'd be breathing funny, and he'd yank at me, hard, almost as if he were angry: *I got you, come on out.* Our parents would sit and talk in the living room and, only because they were family, I wasn't even embarrassed by the music of the crank when I was sent out to grind the coffee. Uncle Melquias's reassuring monotone guaranteed it was Sunday. Life was good, everything was going as expected, marvelous and full of mishaps.

"Some critter's picking off the chickens, we've already lost two, just yesterday morning the chicken coop was a carpet of feathers. If they don't hoe those weeds along the tracks, someone's going to find themselves a little surprise in the form of a rattler. The priests are handing out movie tickets to the kids instead of Catechism books, what's this world coming to? Ah, no, I've had one too many cookies already, but another cup of coffee . . . "

When I tiptoed across the living room pretending to look for something, super-intent on their conversation, they wouldn't even notice me. It was as if they were royalty, the king and queen of a neighboring kingdom come to visit, with all the pageantry and ceremony.

After a few days, Papa would announce that it was time we visited Aunt Efigeninha's, and the ritual began anew: mantras of blessings and salutations, all those ahems, God bless yous, see you laters, and see you soons, until I grew up and married a college graduate and Benedito grew up and married a factory worker. We had children, sorrows, frights, and dreams of a lamppost surrounded by beetles, scraps of reprimands ringing in our ears like the sweetest endearments: *come inside this very minute, you impossible creature, it's time you start behaving like a young lady.* Mama was severe and sorrowful, Papa was always happy: *leave the girl alone, she's getting big but she's still just a kid.*

Today I'm melancholy and sighing a lot, like my mother. It's been raining since morning, water flooding this cellar of memories. They float on the mad torrent rushing along to the river. Let them sail away, I won't lose them. The river is inside me.

Translated by Ellen Doré Watson

Santinha and Me

Adélia Prado

FROM A DISTANCE, it looked to Santinha like the arche-type of a poor house. A half of a half of a house, made of the cheapest cinderblock. Bare of plaster, a slice of house that riveted that little saint completely. She pulled over, got out of the car, and stood staring, enthralled.

The window's shut, said Santinha.

And even so, it looks cross-eyed, I said, thinking about the meadow we had set out to find, a place to sit in silence.

But Santinha found this fraction of a house irresistible.

Come on, she said.

Up to the house? But it's getting late, we have a long drive ahead.

I knew Santinha, and I wanted to derail her from another one of her attacks of generosity, which, to my view, were rooted more in psychology than asceticism.

Listen, I have a fifty in my purse, and I mean to get rid of it.

This is Prado's second story in this collection. For her biographical information, see page 159.

Uh oh, I thought, this is going to be hard, and I reminded her of the need to "practice charity judiciously," as we'd learned in the most recent course we'd taken together, THE PATH TO PERFECTION.

I know, she said, but I am being judicious—that house is incredibly poor and I have more cash than I need, so let's go. I'll just say, here's fifty reais to buy roof tiles and that'll be that.

But the house already has a roof, Santinha.

OK, whatever—tiles, linoleum, wood flooring. . . .

God in heaven! Wood floorboards, for a shack like that? He'd lay down cement is all.

OK, then let him buy cement.

Ai, woman, and what if he gets offended, and tells us to beat it, have you thought of that?

Well, that's his problem, mine is to get rid of this cash.

There's no stopping her, I thought, beginning to catch her enthusiasm.

All right then, let's go.

We had to take the long way around because the street was nearly impassable and on a sharp incline, but finally there we stood in front of that preposterous abode, perched on its steep and rocky lot. A brand new piece of sheet metal had been hung haphazardly in the window hole, leaving a large gap. Beside the door, also made of sheet metal, was a prominent sign bearing the number 900. The owner had planted the drop-off with thick grass, as they do along highways to prevent erosion. Nobody home. Scrawled on the wall, in charcoal: FOR ALL or ONE AND ALL, or something like that. In the scrappy yard, a fenced-in area for a small group of gray rabbits, well-tended with fresh greens. Alongside, a hole in the ground with a bamboo cover, no doubt to trap predators. The gate opened easily, meant only to inspire respect. Which it did, because we entered timidly.

What will we say? I fretted. And what if somebody comes along?

We say we came to ask for a drink of water, or to buy some eggs, said Santinha, fully engaged in the adventure.

I was keeping a nervous eye on the neighbor across the street, who was yelling at his dogs.

Let's forget it, Santinha, look, the house has two television antennas.

Yeah, but they're old and crummy, she said, definitely only for black and white, with lousy reception. They're just for looks.

Well, at least be quick, Santinha, I'm scared someone will come, and besides, the guy will probably think it's a hex or something and burn your money, why not just give it to me instead?

We'll leave a note, she said. Dear sir, this is for you to buy cement.

Do you really want to engineer your gift like that, Santinha? Why not let the man do what he wants with it?

OK, but I can't just leave loose cash, I'll roll it up in a piece of paper.

That's risky, too, I said. What if he thinks it's trash and throws it away?

Ahhh, you're right. Is the guy with the dogs watching? No, he's gone.

Well then. Santinha tore a page out of her address book and pronounced each syllable as she wrote: SIR, THIS IS

FROM YOUR GUARDIAN ANGEL, then crossed out the "Sir." After all, it might be a poor widow who lives here.

She folded the bill inside, leaving one corner showing, and wrote on the front of the paper: A NOTE FOR YOU.

She shoved it under the door, so it wouldn't get wet or stolen, and said, OK, we can leave now, but just look at the yard—papayas, bananas—this family is hard-working.

She was right—theirs was a poverty that was grateful and patient.

You think they're Catholic or Evangelical? asked Santinha.

Hard to tell. Either way, they're pious people, the kind that knows this world is provisional and their true house is planted in a different lot.

Suddenly I felt very, very poor, myself, and it was good.

As we headed back to the car, I thought how, in the middle of this whole drama, when we hesitated, Santinha had said, Don't worry, if something goes wrong, God will make it right.

Translated by Ellen Doré Watson

The Cage

Augusta Faro

BECAUSE MY PLAITS were soft and lustrous, and the skin of my face tasted of velvety fruit, fresh and shot with color, I lay back that day beneath the glass tile in the roof of the cage, in the long hammock laced with the perfume of black homemade soap. This was the beginning of an unfortunate destiny, which branded my forehead and made me drag a part of my heart through life like a lump of hardened meat. Not long after that my hair began to turn gray at the temples and my eyes decided to burrow

AUGUSTA FARO was born in Goiânia, in the state of Goiás, where she still lives. Her work draws from local legend and the oral tradition of Brazil's backlands, in which the fantastic and the absurd rampage through her characters' otherwise uneventful, small-town lives. Faro has published a vast body of literature that includes sixty books of children's poetry, four books of adult poetry, and the collections of short stories *A Friagem* (*The Chill*) and *Boca Benta de Paixão* (*Holy Mouth of Passion*). Several of her stories have been made into short films. She also contributes short stories and chronicles on a regular basis to a number of newspapers throughout Brazil's Central-West.

in, becoming two bluish-green ponds clouded over by the haze from the chimney of the house where I leaned my belly against the edge of the stove while seasoning the children's soup and boiling the milk, because my own milk had dried up early on and I had to use milk from the goats in the large gravelly yard, and also because my great-grandmother, who still spoke and prayed in a shred of a voice and covered herself in a corner of the dark room like a stain in the void, insisted that bright-eyed children with strong teeth should drink goats' milk as their mothers dried up so early, inside and out, because they tore so much marrow and sustenance from the gravy of blood and bones to knead the day of the husband who would come along with his voice raised as if he had been born a king and the flock of children, his first subjects.

And he would run his hand over his mustache and the backsides of the helpers of the sunken-eyed mother who was always pregnant and wilting in silence, and the ticking of the clock changed very little.

In all that confusion, I was no longer sure if I was the one with the soft plaits with large golden streaks or the one hanging on the wall in the oval photograph of my aunt, already old, a black shawl about her shoulders and a very dark mesh covering her eyes, though not her lips, thin because they had stopped smiling too soon.

And the man in boots would arrive ready for lunch, expecting the polished platters to be laid out on the white tablecloth, and the wine shouldn't be long in coming, and they had to be quiet so as not to interfere while he listened to himself chewing, nor interrupt his serious thoughts, because he was the only one in the house who thought, the others being clay puppets, though they served to tend to the bed, the table and his more urgent needs, because the others he could take care of elsewhere, preferably in one of those houses where the girls were neither sad nor happy, but would lie back, perfume always sweetening their fingers, heavy with rings of colored stones, lackluster, because when they washed their children's clothes they often forgot to remove them and leave them on the bedside table next to the cup of lemon-grass tea, calmer of daily nerves.

And time came along, weaving its lace here and there like the curtains on the drawing room windows. And my voice, already little given to speech, shriveled into silence, and as my muteness deepened I became inflexible and forgot the art of conversation. I started napping three times a day, always on one side, because a very tender, painful rose had blossomed on my left side. I took great care not to hurt the flower, for if I did, the flesh of my own body would shudder so deeply that I could have easily slipped on the wooden floor, so heavily waxed it resembled a mirror. My worth and servitude were now greatly reduced and for this reason I took to staying in the dark, though I was not yet half the age of my great-grandmother, who was still alive and prayed and cursed the things that did not please her in a shred of a voice.

As my mother was as dark as an Indian, she never slept and continued her endless needlework with the stealth of dew, making long or colorful doilies to decorate the houses of the entire family. She even mingled with the sunlight that dawned and entered, never interrupting her toil except for a few hours when the silence and the dogs in the dark felt that the night had grown too heavy.

All the chores and labor of life made my veins wither

in my arms and my wrists became so weak that things slithered from my clutch.

Once in a while someone would come into the room and I would hear, "Need something?" but what I needed, no one had ever given me, right from the very first wail of my newborn lungs. But my voice could hardly be coaxed out and those who asked never knew if there would be an answer; either that or they were in a hurry, closing the door behind them, and they wouldn't have heard me even if I had shouted. But I never shouted; in fact, I had rarely shouted even when I was stronger.

That is why I saw myself for the last time in the bedroom mirror, with the look of one who had stumbled into the world by mistake.

The mirror still hangs there, but the windows are open now and the women, daughters of the daughters I carried in my womb, look at themselves in it, but they don't lower their eyes or close their mouths. Quite the contrary; they talk a lot with the other women and their men. I don't even worry any more, it's almost never necessary, because these women have opened the doors and windows, aired out the house, and not all of them lie back beneath that moonlit tile of glass, nor do they swoon like china dolls when they are stroked and caressed. They have opened all of the windows and I see the sun pouring in resolutely, casting lace on the floorboards, and their chirping is so loud that no one shuts them in the cage or hangs it from the highest beam of the veranda as they did with me and many women of my generation and many other generations before I was born.

Translated by Alison Entrekin

Rediscovery

Adriana Lisboa

I RETURN APPREHENSIVELY to Brasília, thirty years later. Maybe Brasília is only a childhood tale in which I hear echoed nonsense words, like superblock, Monumental Axis, and Gilberto Salomão Mall. (I was learning to talk and my mother showed me off to guests by asking: what are we going to do at Gilberto Salomão? To which I responded: play. Until one day when I really needed to go to the bathroom and I gave an unexpected answer.)

Maybe the capybaras were only a dream. But what about that photograph? Me in a hat, my father hugging me, and the soggy brown little animal on the other side of the gate, greeting us. Someone photographed my dream—natural conclusion. Brasília is an imaginary place where I secretly watched *Godspell* on television with my sister. In Brasília I fought with my brother and then spent the whole day afraid of him. Brasília is an imaginary place where dreams can be photographed.

I feel no vertigo as I look through the window of my hotel room, on the nineteenth floor. I see the television tower, which is immense and tiny, like everything in Brasília. Is my hotel in Brasília, in Tokyo, or in Berlin? The men in ties and the women in high heels don't say

This excerpt was taken from *Caligrafias* and is Lisboa's second piece in this collection. For her biographical information, see page 16.

good morning in the elevator. They're all doing business on cell phones, and they meet with important people over breakfast. Because life is urgent. My fellow *Cariocas* show up in flip-flops, speaking loudly in order to show off their accent. Because life is *Carioca*. The men in ties hold the elevator door for me, the *Cariocas* don't.

Brasília plays tricks: in an instant it pulls from its top hat an Enchanted Kingdom School so I can touch my childhood, but I approach cautiously. I don't know if it's the same. From that other one I've held onto my fear of the chubby blond kid and the T-shirt that the teacher painted for me. Brasília gives me no answers. Everything is whispers. There are no sidewalks for the pedestrian and no paths for your gaze, which flutters about like a drunken bird. They say: monumentality. But I'm not struck. Brasília is an epiphany, and it's also a slight yawn made up of small and instantaneous things, of little corners and surprises. Paradox? The norm. There is nothing quite as false as the assumption of coherence, especially in Brasília.

But I continue to feel a bit fearful that at any moment the people will lose all weight and take off, floating among the countless skies of Brasília, finally and irreparably invaded by this space. If I brought questions, Brasília, generous, gave me more questions. Brasília did not return myself to me, it only pointed out to me others (other selves, other Brasílias), that fit within the same imagination. The pulse of my bloodstream also carries cells of concrete, porous, vaporous, a sigh rising from the Central Highlands.

Translated by Malcolm McNee

Geography

Adriana Lisboa

IN THE *CHAPADA* EVERYTHING IS BIG. The sky
ends only when your gaze gives up, or when myopia bests
you. Walk all day and check the map: you've covered only
space enough for your fatigue. The *chapada* challenges
muscle, canteen, camera. The air is excessive and hurts,
drying up your breath in this brownish June. But the water
of the Black River is black and transparent, and your feet
find no reason to be fearful of diving. Your voice finds
no resonance for its cry. To the sky's sublime inquietude
your thought is superfluous. Even your life is superfluous.
The savannah sky dismisses witnesses and the sun sets,
metamorphosis, blue and yellow catharsis in the *canindé*
macaws. Someone said that the mountains here grow
inward. You've fallen into the belly of the earth, where
you're undone as quickly as any bit of food. Skin burns,
the night is cold and the stars pulsate the entire insomniac
galaxy as you die once again.

In the *chapada* everything is small. In a half-meter of

See page 16 for Lisboa's biographical information.

river the fish nibble your feet and the bubbles in the water last just a second. The current mirrors three hundred tiny suns. Three hundred million. Pink in the morning, at noon the *mimosas* are already white. The dust has wings and claws at your hair, and no white of your clothing lasts more than five minutes. Minimal lunar valleys made of rock and sand fit within two strides. In the *chapada* you are the size of your eyes and your laughable ability to startle. In the *chapada* whatever startles you is also the miraculous place of a flower. Of an insect. Of the animal that is only tracks and traces. In the sore muscle of your thigh you find your soul, which pulses, which inverts the circle, which is born again.

Translated by Malcolm McNee

Shaving

Luiz Vilela

THE BARBER FINISHED arranging the towel around the man's neck. He touched him with his hand.

"He's still warm . . ."

"When did it happen?" asked the young boy.

The barber didn't answer. A few grizzled hairs were showing on the dead man's half-open shirt. The boy was watching attentively. Finally the barber looked at him.

LUIZ VILELA, born in Minas Gerais in 1943, won Brazil's National Fiction Prize with his first book of short stories *Earthquake* (1967). In 1973 he won the prestigious Jabuti Prize for his book *The End of Everything*. He has published more than two dozen books, including novels, novellas, and various short story collections. His work has been translated into Spanish, French, Italian, German, Swedish, Polish, Czech, and English. His stories have appeared in *Translation, The Literary Review, Confrontation, Nimrod, Epoch,* and *Southern Humanities Review.* Vilela writes about ordinary people with a combination of irony and sympathy reminiscent at times of Anton Chekhov. "Shaving" reveals his deep compassion for his characters, especially children, bewildered in a world of isolation and loss.

"When did he die?" the boy asked again.

"Late at night," said the barber, "he died late at night."
He reached out his hand.

"The brush and cream."

The boy quickly got the brush and the cream from the
leather case on the small table. Then he took the water
pitcher he had brought with him into the room, poured
a bit into the small cream cup, and stirred till there was
lather. He was always quick at his work, but right now his
speed seemed accompanied by a certain nervousness—the
brush ended up slipping out of his hand and fell, hitting
the leg of the barber, who was seated next to the bed. The
boy apologized with great awkwardness and became even
more agitated.

"It's nothing," said the barber, cleaning the spot of
lather off his pants, "these things happen . . . "

The boy, after picking up the brush, stirred a bit more,
then gave it to the barber, who also stirred some more.
Before beginning the job, he looked at the boy.

"Don't you think it might be better to wait outside?" he
asked politely.

"No, no thank you."

"Death isn't a pleasant sight for the young. Or for
anyone."

He began to lather the dead man's face. The beard, a
four-day growth, was thick.

Through the closed door came a muffled murmur of
voices telling their beads. Outside the sky had turned
light; a fresh breeze entered the room through the open
window.

The barber gave back the brush and the small cup, the

boy was ready with the razor and strop in his hand. He put the cup with the brush on the table.

The barber began to strop the razor. Everyone at the barbershop knew his style of stropping in accompaniment to lively snatches of classical music, which he would whistle. There in the room, at the side of a dead man, he sharpened with a different rhythm, more slowly and evenly spaced; one might almost have supposed that in his head the barber was whistling a funeral march.

"It's so strange," said the boy.

"Strange?" the barber interrupted his stropping.

"Here we are shaving him . . . "

The barber looked at the dead man.

"What *isn't* strange?" he said. "He, we, the dead, the living; what isn't strange?"

He began shaving. He supported the dead man's head with his left hand and began to shave with his right.

"May God help me to die shaven," said the young boy, who already had a bit of beard. "Then they won't have to shave me after I'm dead. It's so strange . . . "

The barber stopped, held the head away from him, and looked again at the dead man's face; but this had nothing to do with the boy's remarks, he was just looking to see how his work was going.

"Could he be watching us from somewhere?" asked the boy.

He looked up—the ceiling with the light still on—as if the soul of the dead man were up there watching them; he didn't see anything, but he felt as if it were there.

The blade was now cleaning up under the chin. The boy stared at the dead man's face, his closed eyes, his mouth, his pale color. Without his beard he looked even more dead.

"Why do people die?" he asked. "Why do people have to die?"

The barber didn't say anything. He had finished the shaving. He cleaned off the razor and closed it, placing it on the edge of the bed.

"Could you give me the other towel," he said, "and wet the cloth."

The boy wet the cloth in the pitcher, then wrung it out. He gave it to the barber along with the towel.

The barber carefully began to clean off and dry the dead man's face. With the tip of the cloth he removed a bit of lather that had gotten into an ear.

"Why don't we get used to death?" asked the boy. "Don't we have to die someday? Doesn't everybody die? So why don't we get used to it?"

The barber stared at him for a moment.

"Exactly," he said, and, turning again to the dead man, he prepared to trim the mustache.

"Isn't it strange," asked the young boy. "I don't understand."

"There are lots of things one doesn't understand," said the barber.

He held out his hand.

"The scissors."

In the house, movement and the sound of voices seemed to have increased; now and then there was a sob. The boy thought with pleasure how they were almost finished and that in a few more minutes he would be outside, walking down the street in the cool morning air.

"The comb," said the barber, "you can start putting things away."

When he had finished combing, the barber got up from his chair and contemplated the face of the dead man.

"Hand me the scissors again," he said.

The boy reopened the case and took out the scissors. The barber bent over and cut the tip off a hair in the mustache.

The two of them stood and looked.

"Death is a very strange thing," said the barber.

Outside, the sun was already bathing the city, as it began to stir for yet another day of work: shops were opening, students walking to school, cars passing by.

The two walked for some time in silence until, at the door of a small bar, the barber stopped.

"Shall we have a little drink?"

The boy looked at him, a bit at a loss; he only drank in secret, and didn't know what to say.

"A little drink is good for the nerves," said the barber, looking at him with a gentle smile.

"OK . . . " said the boy.

The barber put his hand on his shoulder, and together they entered the bar.

Translated by Alexis Levitin

The Misplaced Machine

J. J. Veiga

YOU ALWAYS ASK WHAT is new in this little town of ours and, at last, there is something Big! Let me tell you that we now have a most imposing machine and it makes us all very proud. Ever since it arrived, I can't remember exactly when, I'm not very good at dates, we have hardly talked of anything else; and the way the people here get

---

J. J. VEIGA (1915–1999) is considered the Brazilian father of magic realism. His tales depict ordinary realities impregnated with strange and threatening possibilities. Many of his stories are set in his native Goiás, where he grew up far from the populated coastal region where he lived the last fifty years of his life. His best-known books are *Os Cavalinhos de Platiplanto (The Little Horses of Platiplanto), Hora dos Ruminantes (The Hour of the Ruminants),* and *Sombras de Reis Barbudos (Shadows of Bearded Kings).* He was awarded the Machado de Assis Prize for his complete works by the Brazilian Academy of Letters in 1997. His books have appeared in Norway, Sweden, Denmark, Czechoslovakia, England, Spain, and Portugal. Two of his collections, *The Three Trials of Manirema* and *The Misplaced Machine and Other Stories,* are available in the United States.

---

heated about the most infantile affairs it's a wonder no one yet has started a fight about it (except the politicos, of course).

The machine arrived one afternoon when most families were eating their dinners, and was unloaded in front of the mayor's office. When we heard the shouts of the drivers and their helpers, a lot of us postponed dessert and coffee and went to see what it was all about. As is usual on such occasions, the men were in a bad mood and would not stop to give any explanation; they bumped into the onlookers on purpose, stepped on their feet without excusing themselves, threw the ends of greasy ropes on them. Those who wanted to stay clean and unhurt had to get out of the way.

Once the various parts of the machine were unloaded, the men covered them with a tarpaulin and went off to eat and drink in a tavern in the square. A lot of us townspeople gathered in the doorway to stare, but no one dared approach the strangers because one of them, apparently guessing our intentions, kept filling his mouth with beer and squirting it in our direction. We decided their disdain was probably due to tiredness and hunger and thought it best to leave our unanswered questions for the following day. But when we went by their rooming house early next morning we were told they had put the machine together, more or less, during the night and departed at dawn.

And so the machine remained, exposed to the elements, no one knowing who had ordered it or what it was for. Of course, everyone had an opinion (and gave it freely), but no opinion was more valid than another.

The children, no respecters of mysteries as you know,

tried to take over the novelty. Without asking anyone's permission (and whose would they ask?) they took off the tarpaulin cover and climbed all over the machine. They still do, playing tag among the cylinders and shafts. They sometimes get caught in the gears and scream their heads off until someone comes along to get them out; it's no use fussing, punishing, or spanking, those kids are plainly enamored of the machine.

Contrary to the opinion of some few who denied any enthusiasm and swore that the novelty would wear off in a few days and rust take over the metal, interest has not flagged in the least. Nobody goes by the square without stopping to look at the machine, and each time there is some new detail to notice. Even the little old church ladies passing by at daybreak and evening, praying and coughing, turn toward the machine and bend a knee discreetly, almost, but not quite, crossing themselves. Brutish types, like that Clodoaldo (you know, the one who shows off in the marketplace, grabbing bulls by the horns and throwing them to the ground) even they treat the machine with respect. If occasionally one or another gives the lever a hard tug or kicks at one of the shafts, you can tell it's just bravado, to keep up his reputation.

Nobody knows who ordered the machine. The mayor swears it was not he and says he consulted the files and found no document authorizing the transaction. But apparently he does not want to wash his hands of it completely because, in a way, he took it over when he designated an employee to look after the machine.

We have to admit—actually everyone does—that the employee is doing an excellent job. At any time of day, even occasionally at night, he can be seen clambering over it, disappearing here, reappearing there, whistling or singing, busy and tireless. Twice a week he smears polish on the brass parts, rubs and rubs, sweats, rests, rubs again—and the whole thing sparkles like a jewel.

We are so accustomed to the presence of the machine in the square that if one day it should collapse, or if someone from another town should come to fetch it, proving (with documents) that he had a right to, I have no idea what would happen. I don't even want to think of it. It is our pride and joy—and don't think I'm exaggerating. We still don't know what it's for, but that doesn't matter much. Let me tell you that we have had delegations from other towns, in and out of state, wanting to buy the machine. They pretend not to want anything, they visit the mayor, praise the town, meander around the subject, throw out a little bait, and then show their hand: how much do we want for the machine? Fortunately, the mayor is honest and smart, and doesn't fall for soft talk.

The machine is now part of the festivities on all civic occasions. You remember how holidays used to be celebrated at the bandstand or on the soccer field? Now everything happens near the machine. At election time all the candidates want to stage their rallies in the shade of the machine and as it isn't possible (there are too many), there are always fights. Happily, the machine has not yet been damaged in these brawls, and I hope it won't be.

The priest is the only person who has not paid homage to the machine, but you know how cantankerous he is; he's even worse nowadays, it's his age. In any case, he hasn't yet tried anything, and Heaven help him if he does.

As long as he keeps to his veiled censuring we'll put up with it; that's his business. I heard he had been talking about eternal punishment, but it didn't cut any ice.

The only accident of any importance until now was when the delivery boy from old Adudes' store (spiky little old man, smears brilliantine on his mustache, remember?) got his leg caught in one of the gears of the machine, entirely his own fault. The boy had been drinking at a *serenata* and, instead of going home, decided to sleep on the machine. He managed to climb to the top platform, no one knows how, and in the early morning he rolled off; he fell on the gears and his weight started the wheels going around. The whole town awoke with his yelling; people ran to see what was the matter and had to get bars and levers to stop the wheels that were eating into his leg. Nothing happened to the machine, fortunately. The careless guy, without leg or job, now helps with the upkeep of the machine, looking after the lower parts.

There is a movement afoot to declare the machine a municipal monument—but it is only a movement so far. The priest, as always, is against it, wants to know what it would be dedicated to. Have you ever known such sour grapes?

People say the machine has even performed miracles, but that (just between us) I regard as an exaggeration, and I'd rather not dwell on the matter. Personally, I— and probably the greater number of townspeople—don't expect anything in particular of the machine. It is enough for me that it stays where it is, cheering, inspiring, and consoling us.

My one fear is that, when we least expect it, some fellow will arrive from abroad, a resolute know-it-all type, and will examine the machine inside and out, think a bit, and then start to explain the purpose of it. To show how clever he is (they're always very clever), he will ask at the garage for a set of tools and, disregarding all protest, he will get underneath the machine, start tightening, hammering, coupling, and the machine will start to function. If that happens, the spell will be broken and the machine will cease to exist.

Translated by Pamela G. Bird

Those Lopes

João Guimarães Rosa

A BAD BREED, who make for bad peace: I want to stay far miles from them. Even from my sons, three in number. A free woman, I don't feel old or worn out. Quality comes with age. I love a man, and my good ways make him marvel, his mouth water. My desire now is to be happy, in my day-to-day, whether suffering or celebrat-

JOÃO GUIMARÃES ROSA (1908–1967) is considered Brazil's most difficult and greatest modern writer. His revolutionary treatment of language has led to comparisons with James Joyce and William Faulkner. He was familiar with a dozen foreign languages, studied the grammar of another dozen, and was especially interested in the spoken language of nomadic peoples of the backlands of Minas Gerais and Bahia. His ethnographic and linguistics background enabled him to use syntax and semantics to show us a world far from our own. His book, *Grande Sertão: Veredas*, considered one of the major works of the twentieth century, has so far defied adequate translation. Two collections of his short stories have been translated into English: *Sagarana* and *The Third Bank of the River and Other Stories*. His work has appeared in *Grand Street, The Literary Review,* and *TriQuarterly*.

ing. I want to talk out loud. Let no Lopes come near, or I'll chase him off with bared teeth. What's behind me, all I went through, repeated itself until it was forgotten. At last I found the bottom of my heart. The greatest gift in the world is to be a virgin.

But first it's others who write our story.

As a little girl I saw myself dressed in flowers. But what stands out earliest is poverty. What good were a mom and dad to a monetary orphan? I became a young woman without abandoning innocence: I sang children's tunes crossed with romantic melodies. I wanted to be called Maria Miss, never caring for the name I was named: Flausina.

God gave me this black beauty mark on the whiteness of my chin. I looked pretty even when I saw my face in the trough, in the pigs' swill. And he passed by, Lopes, big hat, brim turned down. They're all good for nothing, but this one, Zé Lopes, was the worst, an arrogant seducer. He looked at me standing there in my helpless trembling, nailed by his gaze.

He passed on horseback, in front of the house, and my dad and mom greeted him, sullen like they weren't with others. Those Lopes were a breed apart, from another riverbank. They bought or seized everything, and if it weren't for God they'd be here to this day, lording it over us. People should be meek, mild, like flower blossoms. Mom and Dad didn't lift a finger to defend me.

Little by little it comes back to me . . .

With barely enough time to weep, I wanted at least a trousseau, like other girls, the illusion of an engagement. What did I get? No courtship and no church. With his hot hands and short arms the man grabbed me and took me to a house, to his bed. But I learned to be shrewd. Muffled my tears. Endured that body.

I did what he wanted: I talked dirty. That's exactly what the devil makes some men want from us: invention. Those Lopes! With them if there's no hay, there's no milk. When he gave me money, I acted nice, I said, "I used to be a two-bit virgin. Now I've got three bits." He liked that. Didn't know I was watching and waiting.

He put a scrawny black woman in the house to keep an eye on me. Miz' Ana. Whom I learned to deceive, finagling accounts, and whom I called godmother and friend. I managed to make life smooth on the outside. It was lying on my back that I felt the world's sordidness, the devil's nightshirts.

No one has no idea what it's like: all night scrunched up on a cot, with the dull weight of the other hemming you in, his stink, his snoring, any one of those things amounting to cruel and unusual abuse. I, a delicate girl, made into a captive, with him always there, smothering me, in the dark. Ruination, the man hatching his hidden thoughts, like one day devouring another—how do I know what perversities he snored? All of this tarnishes a bride's whiteness, infects like a disease, pierces the spirit. As sure as I'm here today in a way I never was before. I got squeezed smaller, and on the wall my fingernail scratched prayers, my hankering after other horizons.

I traced the alphabet. Needed to learn how to read and write. In secret. I began from the beginning, aided by the newspapers used to wrap groceries, and by the kids who went to school.

And the money rolled in.

As far as I could, I managed all he had to my own profit. I saved up. Had titles and instruments put in my name. He, oblivious, was making me rich. And once I gave birth to his son, his trust in me was total, almost. He got rid of Miz' Ana when I trumped up false charges: that she'd goaded me to make carnalities with another man, a likewise Lopes—who soon vanished from life, in nobody-knows-how fashion.

Like they say: he who hears only half understands double.

I became a nest of vipers. In his liquor I put seeds, just a few, from the black calabash tree; in his coffee, liana bark and belladonna. Merely to cool down his rabid desire— I confess to no crime. Liana bark makes a man gentler, more refined. He was already looking yellowish, like an egg just laid by an ostrich. In short order he died. My life was quite lethal. After the funeral I swept the house and tossed out the dust.

And do you think those Lopes left me in peace?

Two of them, tough types, demanded my hand—the cousin and brother of the lately departed. I maneuvered in vain to keep the brutes at bay. One of them, Nicão, set a due date. "Wait for me at the end of the requiem Mass." Which would be in thirty days' time. But the other one, Sertório, lord and master, with gold and dagger in hand, didn't even wait seven days before barging into my house to claim me. I suffered with composure. How did I lead my life? Year after year of submissive subjection, as tiresome as catching rain in a gourd or chopping kale real fine.

Both men raging, oozing with jealousy. And for good reason—I set it up. Nicão kept circling the house. Were the two sons I bore really Sertório's? The sum total, whatever was supposed to be his, I charged, quickly adding it to my account—honor included. I acquired new graces and enjoyed them in the garden of myself, all alone. I assumed a more maidenly air.

Smiling I leaned out the window, lips puckered: negotiable, impartial. Until my idea hardened into action. I knew he was a Lopes: unruly, fiery, water boiling out of the pan. I saw him leave the house, steaming with steam, clothed in fury, his pockets full of slanders. I'd sent the other one messages, coated with sugar. Lately I'd laughed for a definite reason. Good guy against good guy, my lightning bolts faced off amid shots and flashing metal. Nicão died without delay. Sertório lasted a few days. I wept brokenhearted, according to custom, pitied by all: unfortunate woman, two and a half or three times a widow. On the edge of my yard.

But there was still one left. Sorocabano Lopes: the oldest one, loaded with land. He saw me and got me into his head. I accepted with good grace; he was itching for consolation.

I stipulated, "From now on only if thoroughly married!"

So great was his fervor he agreed—which, for a man of his declining years, was like buttoning a button in the wrong hole. And this Lopes I treated very well and much better, fulfilling his desire.

I racked half my brain: I gave him rich, spicy meals and endless hours of pleasure—the guy was sapped dry from so much love and cuddles. All good things are bad and good for us. The one who died, at any rate, was him. And I inherited all he had, without the slightest qualm.

So finally in the end at last I'm avenged. That vile breed is finished. As for my sons, all of them equally Lopes, I gave them money so they could travel their cattle far away from here. I'm done quarreling: I've found love. Those who don't approve can't sway me. I love, truly. I'm old enough to be his mother? Save your breath. I'm no respecter of calendars and dates.

I don't intend to give him free rein over my body. But I'd like, for my own sake, to have some children of another stripe, civilized and modern. I want the good portion I never had, I want sensitive people. What use are money and understanding to me, if I can't settle with my memories? I, one day, was a very little girl. . . . Everybody lives to serve some purpose. Enough of those Lopes!— they turn my stomach.

Translated by Richard Zenith

The Old Ox

Simões Lopes Neto

WHAT A MEAN CREATURE a man is!

Just think of all our cruelties, and tell me I'm not right. I'll never forget what I witnessed one day with my own eyes; the memory has stayed with me, like a sore under a horse's saddle.

It happened out on the ranch that belonged to the Silva

SIMÕES LOPES NETO (1865–1916) is one of the most important writers to hail from Brazil's southernmost state of Rio Grande do Sul, the land of Brazilian *gaúchos*, the fiercely independent nomadic inhabitants who once made a living from smuggling and from the cattle roaming the borderlands. (Today, *gaúcho* simply refers to anyone from Rio Grande do Sul.) This story was originally published in *Contos Gauchescos* (1912). Simões Lopes focuses on the customs of the region, revealing the paradox of the great hospitality of the people coupled with a culture of lawlessness and violence. His stories document, too, the colloquial Portuguese of the nineteenth-century *gaúcho*, with its rich infusion of Spanish, Quechua, and Guarani words and constant allusions to cattle and horse culture.

---

family, political types, always involved in elections and schemes.

Their ranch was just like this one right here, and it had a brook that ran more than a thousand meters long; it's where the family would sometimes bathe. The brook came to a point, near the dry scrub, then made a turn, like a half-moon, where the sands piled up high and formed a steep bank. The woods out there looked liked they had been planted by a gardener: they were full of *guabiroba* and Surinam cherries, guava and *guabiju*. The ground grew thick with so much fallen fruit, a real delight!

That bend in the brook wasn't far from the house, it was within walking distance, but the family would always head out in their cart, drawn by a pair of tame oxen. One of the ladies of the family would steer the oxen with a leather strap, and one of the children would drive the team on with a broken branch.

They were like patient parents, those two oxen. One was called Dourado; its coat was golden brown. The other, Cabiúna, was black, but its right ear was white, with a stripe running down its dewlap.

Those oxen were experts in their daily labor, and when the family started getting ready early in the morning, after some porridge they'd make with milk and manioc flour, and the kids, still chewing their hunks of bread, came out into the yard, and when the servant girls carrying towels and finally the ladies of the house appeared, when the call went out for the oxcart, those oxen had long since lined up against the beam of the cart; there they stood quietly ruminating, ready and waiting for one of the ranch hands to strap them in.

And so the years went by in this way, with the oxen serving the family well.

When winter came, they were left free in the fields, in the sylvan retreat behind the houses. But sometimes, when there was a bit of sunshine, they would come back to the house as if to inquire whether it was warm enough for the folks to go bathing. And when the kids saw the oxen approaching, they'd start squealing and running around happily, raising a racket on account of those animals.

"Look, it's Dourado! Look, it's Cabiúna!"

And one of those mischievous children would find an ear of corn or some squash for the oxen, and they would eat, baring their teeth as they leisurely chewed, their blubbery lips shining with spit, and the children would laugh as they watched.

Well, with the passing of the years, those children turned into young men and women, they got married and had families of their own. But there were always boys and girls and housewives to fill the cart for those old oxen to carry out to the brook.

Early one morning, at the end of summer, one of the oxen had been found dead, all swollen and rigid. Dourado had been bitten by a snake.

And so Cabiúna, who had been Dourado's constant companion, was now alone. He wouldn't wander far from Dourado's body, but kept close, grazing, lying down, ruminating. If you ask me, the bellowing of that old ox—showing now the thick wrinkles of age at the base of his horns—was a sign of his deep longing for his companion, and so he would call out, as he did long ago, for Dourado to graze with him, to drink with him, to pull the cart with him.

You don't believe me? Animals understand each other! They speak with the same tongue.

When Cabiúna would get close to Dourado and sniff that terrible smell, the vultures would hop away, smeared with fetid blood, sometimes even gagging as they vomited pieces of putrid flesh . . . those damned birds!

Since Cabiúna remained all alone, the family had to look for another team of oxen, and so the old ox would spend his days just hanging around the ranch. He began to grow thin. And so much like a grief-stricken person, one who prefers to keep to himself, the ox—filled with sorrow, too, who knows?—wandered out into the woods.

But on a day bright with sun, the old ox reappeared in the yard.

There was a lot of commotion among the children.

"Look, it's Cabiúna! Good old Cabiúna!"

And the ladies came to the door, wives and mothers now, women who once were young girls themselves carried along by Cabiúna. And the boys, now grown men, appeared too, and all of them cried out:

"Cabiúna! Hey, Cabiúna!"

One of them made a comment regarding the skinniness of the ox; another confirmed it; still another said that the ox wouldn't make it through the winter; and so they began to discuss the matter. The first of these men, an impulsive individual, thought it would be best to put the ox down. It had such thick wrinkles there at the base of its horns, showing its age, and it wouldn't put on any weight, and in any case, it would probably die soon, mired in a ditch somewhere . . . it would be unfortunate, to lose all of that leather.

And so they called for one of the farm hands to bring out the lasso, and he came and tied the rope around the ox's neck. The ox followed behind him, like a dog on its leash.

The oxcart itself was near at hand, old and detached, the main beam sticking up in the air, leaning against a post.

The farm hand took out his knife and, with a sudden blow, buried it to the hilt deep into the base of the neck of the gentle ox. When he drew back his knife, there came with it a foaming fountain of blood that gushed from the animal's heart.

A silence fell over everyone who was watching.

The old ox realized he was injured, felt the pain of his wound . . . who knows, maybe he thought this was some kind of punishment, the stinging slap of a rider's rod hitting him too hard, a reprimand for not being ready at the cart. Believe me when I tell you what happened next: he started blowing bubbles of blood from his lips, wheezing as he tried to breathe, but the old ox staggered forward, then leaned his body against the beam of the cart and put his head into the yoke. He was ready, waiting for the farmhand to strap him in, to put on his reins.

The ox got down on his knees. Then he fell and died.

The mutts on the ranch started licking the blood staining the grass; one lifted its leg and pissed on the dead animal lying there. And while the farmhand sharpened his knife to begin butchering the ox, a small boy appeared, fair-skinned and chubby, with curly locks, eating a sweet potato. He approached the dead beast, put a bit of potato in its mouth and tapped one of its horns, speaking the way children do:

"Eat a widdle food, Cabiúna! Don't you be stubborn, Cabiúna!"

And the innocent child laughed, looking up at the adults who stood around, not saying a word, the devils! If you ask me, they felt guilty for the cruel thing they had done to that old ox, who had carried all of them, so many times, out to the brook to bathe and to eat the fruit of the trees that grew there.

Such a rich family, but look how shameless—and all for a bit of leather from that old ox.

What a mean creature a man is!

Translated by Johnny Lorenz

A Barbecue Story

Moacyr Scliar

YOU, MY FRIEND, ask me to explain Rio Grande do Sul in a few words. A hard thing, a tourist thing. Tourists are like that, they always want to know everything, and really fast, in just a few words. Then they return home, to São Paulo, in your case, show the photos and tell their friends what they saw. They speak with authority, as if they know everything there is to know about this immense state,

---

MOACYR SCLIAR (pronounced "skleer") was born in 1937 in Brazil's southernmost state, Rio Grande do Sul. A doctor specializing in public health, he is considered the premier Judeo-Brazilian writer of the 20th century. His novel *The Centaur in the Garden* was named by the National Yiddish Book Center as one of the 100 best books on a Jewish theme in the last 200 years. His more than seventy books include novels, short stories, essays, and historical studies. Elected to the Brazilian Academy of Letters, he has more work translated into English than any Brazilian writer except Jorge Amado. This story, with its delightful regional flavor, was written specifically for this anthology. It demonstrates qualities characteristic of his short fiction: accessibility, terseness, and humor.

---

which has a long and glorious history. But I'm not complaining, my friend. That's the way things are, what can you do? Let's see if I can satisfy your request.

If I had to sum up *gaúcho* culture in a single word, do you know what that word would be, my friend? Barbecue. Yes, I know you're familiar with barbecues. These days there are barbecue restaurants everywhere, São Paulo, Rio, even the United States. Or rather: there are places that call themselves barbecue restaurants and attempt to prepare barbecue. But it's a mere imitation, my friend. A bad copy. True barbecue, that's here, in the land of the gaúcho.

The gaúcho is a meat-eater par excellence. And he had to be a meat-eater, because raising cattle was the first great economic activity in Rio Grande. The pampas, this immense plain, this vast territory won at great cost from the Spanish, was divided into large landholdings where cattle roamed free. The gaúcho ate meat morning, noon, and night. They would slaughter a steer, cut it up, stick the slices of meat onto a spit made from a tree branch, and roast the meat over a bonfire right there in the open. Roast is a figure of speech: the Indians, for example, would eat the meat almost raw, with the steer still bellowing, as they say around here.

Over time all that changed. Making barbecue became a true ritual. It was something I learned as a child and even today—and I've lived 73 good years—I haven't forgotten. And you know why I haven't forgotten? Because the one who taught me how to make barbecue was my grandfather, Colonel Picucha, one of the great ranchers of Rio Grande do Sul, a famous man in the border territory.

Famous for his courage, famous as a political leader—no mayor in the region took office without his blessing—but famous also for the barbecue he made.

He was a master, my grandfather. I learned everything about barbecue from him. I learned how to choose the meat, for example. To him, the best part of the animal was the ribs.

And he would explain: "It's not tender meat, but who wants tenderness? Who wants things easy? Your teeth have to fight the gristle, have to show it who's boss. Like everything in life."

Once the fire was ready (always on the ground; my grandfather disdained grills, believing they were for city slickers) and the ribs were on the metal spit (not a tree branch), my grandfather would season the meat. Not like the French, who use a little of this, a little of that—a girlish thing, according to my grandfather. No, he used only salt. Lots of salt, coarse salt. Again, he didn't want refined salt, restaurant-type salt. No. It had to be coarse.

"Coarse like me," he would say, laughing. "I'm proud of being coarse."

Another rule he always followed: barbecue could only be meat. Anything made with dough, for example, he rejected outright: it was a foreigner's thing, from the Italian settlers—and my grandfather had nothing but contempt for the settlers, confined to their small parcels of land in the mountainous areas. It's true, Brazil needed immigrants, needed people to populate the South, but as he said, "Me here, them there."

My grandfather didn't lack for enemies. Political enemies, mostly. Politics in that region was a violent thing, and the fights between groups frequently ended in lots of deaths—a cut throat was the classic method of getting rid of adversaries. Well, the worst enemy of my grandfather was another landowner, Colonel Batista, known for his courage and his cruelty. But the cause of the rivalry between my grandfather and Colonel Batista wasn't politics. It was barbecue.

For many years the two men had vied for the title of best barbecue cook in the region. In the beginning it was a cordial rivalry, but little by little it became transformed into an open feud. Finally, they decided to hold a kind of contest between the two of them. They would both prepare ribs, which would be served to three other colonels, all of them connoisseurs of barbecue. They would be the judges in the contest. Their decision would be final.

The day of the contest, which took place at the home of a mutual friend, arrived at last. Separated by a prudent distance, each one lit his fire. They prepared their respective ribs, stuck them onto spits, and roasted them. The judges waited in the house. Finally, two servants appeared, each bearing a cooked rib on a plate; it wasn't known which was Picucha's, which was Batista's. The guests tried one, tried the other, said that both were very good, but, by a vote of two to one, the rib won that was later revealed to be my grandfather's.

Colonel Batista was furious. He had no grounds for complaint, because the contest had been clean, but he considered it a personal insult and swore to get revenge against my grandfather.

And, grabbing the metal spit on which he had cooked his rib, he exclaimed, "And this will be the weapon of my vengeance!"

No one really understood what Batista meant by that. His friends, and several were there, tried to calm him down and even tried to mediate a reconciliation with my grandfather. But the man wouldn't hear of it. He left there foaming with rage.

Time passed, and the fight was all but forgotten. One rainy Sunday, my grandfather was cooking barbecue, by himself, in the shed on his ranch (because of the bad weather), when suddenly the door opened and there stood Colonel Batista, holding the spit on which he had barbecued his ill-fated rib.

"I said I'd get my revenge, Picucha!" he shouted. "And here I am, like a good gaúcho, to keep my word."

My grandfather looked at him calmly and said nothing.

"Defend yourself!" bellowed Batista. "Pick up your spit and defend yourself!"

"I'm using all my spits for the barbecue," Granddad said calmly. "Am I going to have to spoil this rib because of you?"

Batista burst out laughing.

"That's one rib, Picucha, you'll never eat. Because I'm going to put an end to you, right here and now."

Without a word, my grandfather picked up one of the metal spits. He removed the meat from it and threw it onto the fire.

He carefully cleaned the spit and said, "I'm ready. But I want to warn you of something: I'm not going to kill you, Batista. Even though you deserve it, I'm not going to, because you're crazy and don't know what you're saying. But you won't leave here unpunished. With the tip of this spit I'm going to carve a B in your forehead. B for barbecue. B for beef. And when I'm done you're going to leave through that door and disappear from here. For good."

They took their positions, as if wielding swords, and the duel quickly began.

What a battle that must have been, my friend, what a battle. No one witnessed it, but it must have been the fiercest and most frightening thing ever, the spits clanging as they clashed.

They say the duel didn't last long. With the sword, the machete—and the spit—my grandfather was much better than his adversary. In an abrupt move, he managed to wrest the spit from his opponent's hand and, as Batista stood there, dumbfounded, he carried out his promise: he carved the letter B on his forehead. Then he handed Batista a cloth to stanch the bleeding.

And pointing to the door, he ordered, "Get out!"

Colonel Batista left. And was never seen again. He emigrated to Uruguay and did not come back. A rancher who ran into him by chance said that Batista used a brimless hat and a bandana on his forehead, no doubt to hide the B-shaped scar.

That's the story, my friend. The story of my grandfather Picucha, from whom I learned how to cook meat. Speaking of which, wouldn't you like to have some barbecue with me? No? Ah, you're in a hurry. People from São Paulo are like that, always rushing. We'll leave it for next time, then. There'll always be a rib waiting for you here. Prepared on a spit, of course.

Translated by Clifford Landers

Loss

Pena Cabreira

For the writer Guido Kopittke

WHEN I GOT THE NEWS that my old painter friend
had died, the vertical world of my mind was turned upside
down. I plunged into his horizontal universe. Not because
today his body is motionless in that position, but because
Arthur lived a great part of his life on the immense
straight, flat line of the largest beach in the world, in the

Pena Cabreira was born in 1953 in the state of Rio Grande do
Sul. In his own words he "draws, paints, and writes when he
can and needs to." His story "The Platform," which has been
compared to Shirley Jackson's "The Lottery," appeared in *Words
Without Borders*. This is his second work to be published in
English. "Loss" evokes a feeling of the remoteness of a distant
corner of land's end at the farthest tip of the vast Brazilian
subcontinent. Just as Brazil is a land of contrasts, so too is Rio
Grande do Sul, ranging from modern, cosmopolitan urban
centers like capital Porto Alegre to the seemingly endless grass-
lands of the pampas. Cabreira presents in stark juxtaposition
the age-old struggle between enlightenment and superstition,
and between art and obscurantism, with the bleak, indifferent
landscape as silent witness.

extreme south of Brazil, in contrast to my urban existence, surrounded by the tall, upright buildings of Porto Alegre. An enormous repentance at not having looked him up in the last twenty-something years opened before me like an abyss. I sank into a great sadness and felt that a true part of me was about to disappear forever. My mind did a rapid balance sheet of my life, illustrated with distant visions of my youth. Things and friends, lost . . . I slept badly, dreamed of the stormy and muddy sea of Albardão and Arthur's voice speaking of a deranged woman who lived at the edge of the beach and made sacrifices to the sea. I awoke several times during the night and the dream would return, ever more violent, the noise of the sea and Arthur's voice becoming a single thing, powerful, dense, incomprehensible. At five AM, flooded with fear and soaked in sweat, I decided not to close my eyes again.

I got out of bed with my mind made up I would go south to recover memories of Arthur and unearth the reality of the woman in the dream. I needed to try to contact the submerged part of my life. If I didn't take advantage of that chance, I would always feel guilty. Time offers us windows now and then, rare and necessary, that allow us to look at our own life as if it were someone else's, and this was beyond doubt one of them.

I made a series of phone calls to cancel my commitments and began to select the photographic equipment for the journey. This practical task caused me uncommon discomfort; visiting the past as a professional photographer would be to invade my own life without authorization. Breaking into a fragile trunk instead of using the proper key. I rummaged through the storage area with all its drawers, and inside a dusty case found the old Pentax K1000, the first camera bought with my own money. With it I had recorded our adolescence, my first photo essays: shots of a Pelotas both neoclassical and decadent, proud of its colonial past, ennobled by the dried beef cured by the hands of slaves. A unique city, its history preserved by the families of impoverished ranchers and by blacks who never forgot, and whose venerable architecture was colored in the seventies by a generation of hippies tripping out on marijuana and mushrooms. Those were the images of my first exhibition, a symbol of rebellion in the lobby of the Sete de Abril theater, the oldest in Rio Grande do Sul. Of my comrades from that time, few remained in Pelotas. I came to Porto Alegre for college and professional advancement, and Arthur went into isolation along the cold, inhospitable southern coast. Until the eighties I still visited him with a certain frequency, keeping up with his search for a pictorial identity, themes and a color palette. Afterwards, never again.

That Pentax was my emotional bridge. It would be my travel companion and safe conduct to a past seldom visited.

After carefully cleaning and lubricating the old machine and making sure it was once again ready to be the faithful extension of my gaze, from the window of the apartment above Avenida Duque de Caxias I took several snapshots of the river that surrounds the city. We were attuned: brain, vision, and my good camera. My backpack crammed with winter clothes, I descended the stairways of the Borges viaduct with adolescent excitement, and headed toward the Rosário Gallery, where I bought an unnecessarily large supply of film of various speeds. In the garage I got the jeep and headed south. The gigantic vertical sculptures of the city began to shrink and lose importance as I crossed the Guaíba river bridge. Destination: Santa Vitória do Palmar, not far from the state capital in terms of the planet's proportions, but an exhausting and endless trip considering the straightness of the highway, the speed limit, and my impatience. The Rio Grande pampas imposed on me their time and their horizon.

When I arrived in the town, the car refueled, I lost no time in seeking out Hermenegildo Beach. Reaching the sea, I turned left toward Albardão and its lighthouse, the most deserted spot on the Brazilian coastline. En route, the Minuano, our polar wind, bringing heavy clouds and a fine rain, fused sea and sky. It was the region's nature greeting an outsider; I felt important and rejected. I faced a difficult, unstable ground. I discovered it was the "Conchário," fifty kilometers of shifting sand covered with broken shells of every size: a seasonal phenomenon, still little studied, of that beach. I stopped to photograph that unusual scene and was almost unable to leave. Thank heaven the car was getting good traction. I came to the conclusion that I wasn't welcome. Little by little, a perpendicular icon began to take form, the Albardão lighthouse, imposing and unique, anchored in the feminine curves of the sand dunes.

The painter's atelier/home was some three hundred meters from the lighthouse. Parking the car a respectable distance away, I continued on foot. Carrying only the camera and its accessories, I clapped my hands as I entered through the open door. No one. The place was still the same: below, a single space that was living room, kitchen, and studio, enormous windows with a splendid view of the sea; above, the mezzanine with its single bedroom and a window facing north toward the lighthouse. It was all very rustic, built with wood from fishing boats, ropes, and ironwork from ships: the stuff of shipwrecks. The benches and sofas, carved from rough wood, once covered in sheepskin, were now naked. The atmosphere that had once been well lit and cozy was now dark and desolate. With a sudden sensation of opportunity, I took out my Pentax and began to photograph the house from every angle, taking advantage of the magnificent chiaroscuro softened by the subdued bad-weather light. I approached the corner used to paint, shooting the way a soldier pulls the trigger when he enters dangerous territory: quickly, cautiously, precisely. Easel, brushes, palettes, spatulas, small pots and tubes of paint. The artist's colors were limited: brown, sepia, gray, and green. The tones, rich and varied. The lenses captured every detail. Behind the easel bench was an infinity of canvases of several sizes, turned toward the wall. They were magnificent seascapes with the solid structure and diaphanous abstraction of a Turner but with the inalterable, disturbing horizontal expanse there at land's end. With a feeling of heresy and urgency, I set the Pentax up on the tripod and, placing the paintings one by one on the easel, went about making the presentations. I was merely the mechanical arm that carried out the function. The camera and the canvases exchanged silent and profound perspectives. Perennial.

Fascinated by what I was doing, I had lost track of time,

when out of nowhere I was suddenly attacked. Someone
had leapt onto my back and dug their nails into my neck,
howling like a crazed animal. I tried to push aside the
arms that were strangling me, but the person's body was
glued to mine like a barnacle on the hull of an old boat.
I whirled around the room in a desperate dance trying
to free myself of that abrupt and aggressive cargo, until,
nearly strangling, I lost my balance and fell backward
onto the heavy wooden bench. When I got to my feet, I
saw the small body of a woman curled up on the bench.
There was a mournful sobbing, and her enormous dark
eyes stared at me in terror. Cautiously, I sat down beside
her, asked her forgiveness for having invaded her house,
explained who I was and what I was doing there. Her gaze
devoured me. The woman spoke the mixture of Spanish
and Portuguese typical of the region, nonstop and dis-
jointed. I managed to understand that she had been the
last companion of Arthur, suffered at his death, and that
without him nothing any longer made sense. I listened
impatiently to the poor woman's litany, waiting for the
right moment to speak of the fate of the works, when she
broached the exact subject from a disheartening angle.
My friend's paintings were to be destroyed beside the sea,
and only in this way would his spirit rise to heaven. After
all, he had spent his life capturing the ocean through his
art, and therefore his soul now belonged to her. That mys-
tical logic was absurd but irrefutable given her faith. I saw
the Holy Office in the eyes of that fanatical woman, and
human complexity once again succumbing to the Inquisi-
tion. I felt helpless. I remained silent for an eternity of
two minutes, which she perceived as fervent respect. A

valuable advantage in that game of peculiar logic. It was time enough for me to reorganize my thoughts and risk the only move that occurred to me: I argued that every great artist had a divine mission and that her husband's was to spread respect for that sea by his representation of it. So it would be necessary to perpetuate the collection of seascapes in a museum in Santa Vitória do Palmar, in order that no one would ever go to the coast and stand before that immensity without having first understood it through the vision of Arthur, the man who loved that place like no other. I also explained that the paintings shown to the public would always belong to her, for they were her legacy.

I said that and fell silent. Then, for the first time, I saw the hint of a glow in her gaze. I took that as permission and continued. I proposed taking one of the canvases to the local secretary of culture and discussing the possibility of creating the "Arthur Catulo Peres Museum," given the quality and importance of his art for the region. The smile that lit up her long-suffering face and a nod of her head were enough for me to choose an expressive canvas from the collection and drive the car to the city. First, I assured her vague and distant gaze that I would return as quickly as possible.

At the city hall in Santa Vitória do Palmar things went better than expected. The secretary received me and was sympathetic to the case. He knew of the eccentric painter isolated in Albardão. Better still, he was enthralled by the painting, and when he heard that there were hundreds as good or better than it, agreed to the creation of a cultural center to house the entire collection. He would take charge of the project to get funding and assure the backing of the community for the building, and I would try to find supplementary support from large corporations in the capital through my professional contacts.

On my way back, a sliver of sun rose on the horizon. I was pleased at having done something for my old partner, even belatedly. But I felt special pleasure when I thought about his wife, who would proudly be the one responsible for the memory of a great artist who would finally be recognized. A good reason to live.

But my happiness vanished. In the distance, black smoke was effacing the clean line of the beach. My heart raced and my foot pressed down on the accelerator. The scene at the edge of the sea was chilling, and I hated myself for my naïveté. The widow, dressed in rags, was dancing around a crackling fire fed by all the canvases painted by my friend. It was a desperate ritual intended to save her lover's soul.

That brief ray of light, our dream, had come to an end.

Today, when I grow weary of the concrete, vertical world, I return to my own private horizon, Arthur's last surviving painting.

The Pentax is stored in its case and the exposed rolls of film are lying somewhere, forgotten in a box.

Translated by Clifford Landers

The Flying Man

Rodrigo de Haro

The Bird—oh poor mortals!
Shades called men, hear:
we, the birds, were greater
than the Gods . . .

ARISTOPHANES
(from *The Birds*)

A MAN DECIDED TO FLY from off the tower of the
bridge. He set the date, named the hour, and, followed by
a punctual crowd, dragging along his enormous wings of
black cloth, he spoke of the dizziness of flight, of grazing

RODRIGO DE HARO, born in 1939 in Paris, lives in his
rambling house and studio high above a former shrimp-fishing
village on the island of Santa Catarina. The son of the painter
Martinho de Haro, he is a writer of poetry and short fiction
and an artist whose murals and mosaics grace public build-
ings in the capitals of Rio Grande do Sul, Santa Catarina, and
Sao Paulo. His books of poetry include *Pedra Elegiaca, Caliban,
Livro dos Naufagios,* and the more recent *Livro da Borbeleta
Verde.* His poems have appeared in magazines including *Green
River Review, International Poetry Review, Paintbrush,* and
Poetry NOW. This story, set in Florianopolis, reveals de Haro's
inclination toward surrealism and fantasy, linking him to Latin
America's artistic movement of magic realism.

---

the highest treetops with his feet together, of mounting higher and higher, he and his wings, alone.

"To fly is clarity," he said. "All honest dreaming follows a path in the air. Who has never seen himself before an ecstatic landscape? Nobody. We know that our dreams are the rememberings of winged creatures, almost the only ones. Let us fly!"

That's how the aeronaut held forth, more or less, and the crowd followed him, breathless, trampling on one another. I remember: it was a Sunday of sunshine many years ago. Everyone was rushing in excited waves, block-like cars, those sprightly little cars. I reached the head of the bridge from where I could make out the soldier in his sentry box. I looked at the sky, balloons were rising, a small airplane was circling, a windmill in the air. But the heavens were empty—even if space ships were to penetrate outer space, parachutes to fall, a shower of colored ticker tape to float down, mysterious packages to descend in a steady stream from high above the sea—yet the heavens would remain empty without the flying man.

The things of heaven are only on Earth, heaven always recedes, with its angels. All is empty. I remember: heaven doesn't exist, that's what I discovered all of a sudden. One sees that one doesn't see. If I reach it, it isn't heaven. Space, impenetrable thing!

The flying man continued on in front of me, his shadow on the ground, pulling along on an open cart two wings, his accoutrements. Nothing yet fluttered in the ether. What a recompense for death! The heavens! He would be there. Now or afterward? But not being there yet, he did not yet exist. Neither his legs which walked, nor the delicate urn of his cranium existed; was it only heaven then that existed? Was it all heaven: a human urn, the parachute, a herd, the crowd, the air? And if the birdman were against heaven, would he be against himself? What curve in the air would his wings embrace? What spark might suddenly melt the first speck in the air? To fly. To fly.

And gently flying, in stellar space, what precious heavens would recede unto the first heaven?

Watching, I lingered, mouth agape, eyes perhaps glassy. Somebody laughed, plucked at my sleeve. The crowd drew back, full of murmurs. And then I saw, agile, slow, the man who was climbing up and the many arms supporting him, and he climbed up the tower, along the steel pipes, with bare feet, and then no arm could reach him. Next to me, a little boy was afraid that, lost in thought, I had seen nothing, and he tugged at me again. Yes, I remember him, little Adrianino. His father, a famous doctor, was obliged, a bit later, to leave the island: an insect associated with an Amazonian plant was spreading disease throughout the towns along the river and, together with other scientists, he was called away to study the epidemic. Adrianino drew boats and skeletons.

"Are you watching?"

"Heaven doesn't exist," I shot back, angered.

"I know," he said, "heaven is kind of like a step (and he laughed, the smart-aleck, without turning away his squinting eyes). Then, in a murmur, "Could thought be heavier than air? If not, the man will fly."

He was wearing his favorite outfit: knickers, red suspenders, a tie with an anchor on it, a jersey.

The flying man, already high up, stopped, turned his head, and the wings, magnificent, diseased, solemnly swayed. He bent down and spoke, gesturing with his free hand. If we had heard him, would we have understood him? A gust of wind carried off his weak laugh. I remember: so very high, what a sharply etched face that flying man had. The laughter grew, that crazy man. His absurd discourse that we couldn't hear.

A little cloud covered the sun, just for a moment. Immobile, he waited, bowed down. His mouth filled with emptiness formed an arc, and over his eyes (what clarity!) raised eyebrows rendered a fright so exciting that we applauded enthusiastically, tossed our caps in the air, and, creatures that we are, danced.

Then he ran, that man who could no longer come down, that man heavier than air, a quadruped, a butterfly—he ran right up to the top of the tower. What an act that was! What a wild scene! The whole show, the preparation, the lesson, and the consequence: little more than half an hour.

And there at the top he raised his wings, and they unfurled, exalted sails. There was a silence. It was now. At my side, the eyes of the boy glistened with tears. For a moment, everything glistened with tears. For a moment, everything glistened; the flying man leaped into space.

Later on, I received a letter from Adrianino in Amazonas. He spoke of that river I still hadn't seen, of carnivorous plants, and of his butterfly collection. He spoke of a black butterfly with the face of a skull and of the flying man with his livid face who had lost his reason jumping from the bridge on our island.

When he leaped, it was as if he hesitated in the air. The grievous wings fluttered erratically. He spun over, his legs kicking, and slowly began to descend. He described a circle, climbed again, the wings out of sync, his weight great, the sea there below. In a moment the two bays were full of boats, their engines proudly revving. The man was flying, the man was flying! Instead of falling, the fatal outcome of which everyone had been whispering, he flew, and no one budged. He flew, heavily and without a propeller, with no more wrappings than his clothes, the falcon.

He set himself to drawing in space, as the buzzards do on a windy day, very small up there above. He made a figure eight, geometric shapes, beautiful arabesques. And suddenly he disappeared in the air, swallowed up in space, without even a cloud nearby. He climbed and climbed and then disappeared. In the plaza, at the head of the bridge, we were silent, we were like the blind when they stare without seeing the light of the sun. And what if we had had to stay there forever and he had never come back again? What kind of sleep, imprudent ones, would we have slept in the face of a fact so inexplicable?

"He'll come back," smiled the boy. "He went up and he'll come back, he went too high, he entered heaven."

We waited a short while. We waited? We didn't wait at all: we trembled, laughed, wrung our hands, a woman gave birth in a car, the child's wailing spread all over the plaza.

"There he is!"

The blind came to themselves again. Like a dot, an atom of dust, coming straight down, the flying-man fell, his wings destroyed. We ran to see, not wanting to see. It was a dreadful fall. And he fell, right into the sea, without wings, without feathers. The men in a motorboat picked him up, the language he was speaking was unintelligible to them.

"The wings?" asked Adrianino.

The wings were never found.

Translated by Alexis Levitin

The Elephants' Graveyard

Dalton Trevisan

THERE IS A DRUNKARDS' GRAVEYARD in my city. Way at the back of the fish market and on the bank of the river there is an old inga tree—the drunkards are happy there. People think of them as sacred animals and provide them with their necessities of cane liquor and fish with manioc mush. For their regular diet they content themselves with leftovers from the market.

When their stomachs growl so much that it disturbs their napping, they leave their shelter and, dragging their heavy feet, fling themselves into the struggle for life. They

---

DALTON TREVISAN, born in Curitiba in 1925, is perhaps Brazil's most prolific and controversial short story writer. The titles of his forty collections reveal his darkly sardonic view of humanity: *Knife in the Heart, Conjugal War, Crimes of Passion, Disasters of Love, Those Damned Women, My Darling Killer, Death in the Square, The Great Deflowerer,* and his most famous collection, *The Vampire of Curitiba.* His works suggest that beneath the orderly surface of our bourgeois society lies a world of violent passions, selfishness, depravity, and despair.

sink up to their knees in the mangrove swamp hunting for crabs, or, lifting up their red trunks, they watch for a ripe inga to fall.

They know that they are condemned like badly wounded elephants, and they scratch their sores without complaint as they sprawl among the roots that serve as beds and chairs, drinking and nibbling on some piece of fish. Each has his own place, and they politely warn each other:

"Don't use Pedro's root."

"He left, didn't you know?"

"He was here a while back . . ."

"That's right, he felt he was going to snuff out and he took off. I hollered: 'Go ahead, Pedro, and leave the door open.'"

The muddy surface of the swamp has bubbles on it—a lost giant's steps? João puts his fish wrapped in banana leaves onto the coals.

"Did Bellywhopper bring the worms?"

"Didn't you know?"

"Just now he . . ."

"He gave me the can and said, 'Jonas, try to catch some red weakfish.'"

A dying elephant arrives in port from other shores.

"Come join us, friend."

They give him a root of the inga tree, a mug of cane liquor, and a fish tail.

In the silence the buzzing of the mosquitoes shows where each one is posted. Sitting among the roots, they are in awe at the mystery of the night—the lighthouse as it blinks on the top of the bluff.

One of them amuses himself by sinking his finger into

his swollen ankle; he gets up, and dragging his pachyderm feet, he goes off among farewells—spoken in a low voice so as not to disturb the dozers. The latter, when they awaken, don't have to ask where the missing person went. And if they asked, intending to bring him a bunch of daisies from the swamp, what could anyone tell them? Each person's path is revealed to him at the hour of death.

The afternoon breeze stirs up the botflies that stick to their deformed feet, and the leaves of the inga tree are flashing like silvery *lambari* fish—with the sound of falling fruit, the nearest drunkards laboriously get up and fight among themselves, rolling in the dust. The winner peels the inga and sucks the sweetish core with a greedy look. Blood never flows in the graveyard—the small knife at the waist is for scaling fish. And in brawls they are incapable of movement—it is sufficient for them to curse at rowdies from a distance.

And those who suffer from delirium, pestilence, the bitterness of gall upon their tongues, the muggy weather, the blood cramps, roar with obtuse hatred at the sparrows active up in the trees, who spit upon their heads before they sleep—the restless chirping is a poison to their drowsiness.

On the shore they watch the fishermen dipping their oars.

"Have you got a few fish, buddy?"

The fisherman throws them the fish he has discarded in the bottom of his boat.

"What makes you drink, Baitsucker?"

"A mother's curse, what the hell."

"Doesn't Chico want some fish?"

"Poor guy, he died of dropsy."

With the haste his swollen feet allow him, he takes leave of his companions dozing along the bank, forgetting to bait their hooks.

Spitting the black inga seeds out into the water, the others ask him no questions: the ivory tusks pointing the way are empty bottles. Chico disappears into the sacred graveyard among the skeletons of grotesque feet that rise up in the moonlight.

Translated by Gregory Rabassa

Alice and the Writer

Cristovão Tezza

"WRITERS ARE NOT GOOD PEOPLE. What intrigues me is how the thousands of readers still left in the world, like yourselves, you well-meaning souls in the audience there listening to me, don't realize this simple, universal truth. Not satisfied with merely reading the books we write, you also want to hear us speak, you line up for auto-

---

One of Brazil's foremost contemporary novelists, CRIS-TOVÃO TEZZA was born in 1952 and lives in southern Brazil. He has published thirteen novels, including *The Eternal Son*, which won every major literary prize in Brazil in 2008 and is being translated into seven different languages. The recipient of the Brazilian National Library Award in 1998 and the Brazilian Academia of Letters Award in 2004, he teaches Portuguese at the Universidade Federal do Paraná and has published textbooks and numerous magazine and newspapers articles. Rich in nuance and the intimate observation of human behavior, he transports readers into his characters' most private thoughts, where nothing is censored and everything is constantly re-examined. He is presently working on a book of short stories based on the eponymous heroine in "Alice and the Writer."

---

graphs, and some of you listen to us with an adoration befitting saints and wise men. Happy, smiling, you attend lectures and round tables where the writers generally trot out a string of nonsense and lies, always the same ones, harebrained theories that they invented, hungover, fifteen minutes before taking to the podium or which they drag through life like a tablet of commandments that bears no relation to what they write (or, much worse, theories that lamentably *do* bear a relation to what they write), jokes that aren't funny (writers are almost always—paradoxically—individuals devoid of humor), pathetic attacks of narcissism or just twaddle about their 'writing method,' the value of 'inspiration,' the importance of reading in the modern world—soon they'll bring out something like 'how to make friends writing books.' The novice poet and the venerable Nobel Prize winner, they all subject their pathetic selves to the ridicule of speaking in public and their drivel is all the same. There must be exceptions, of course—but I'm not aware of them. Readers are credulous—they believe what is written and they believe in those who write. Those who write have 'the gift.' And that's where we go to town. No one realizes that the raw material of literature is contempt. What irritates me, when I look at myself, is this unctuous dependence on other people, not to survive, which would be fair enough, but to feed off them, because if I weren't surrounded by stupidity I'd have nothing to say and would die completely useless. It'd be one thing if writers could live on their own, in peace—but no, most live in warring groups and tribes, bicker over every centimeter of press coverage, suck up to social columnists, fight desperately for five-

minute radio interviews, and would kill their mothers
for two seconds on television; they take refuge in cliques,
churches, and splinter groups, protect themselves in an
infinite array of lobbies: the gay lobby, the heterosexual
lobby, the feminist, the Jewish, the Arabic, and the com-
munist lobbies; the lesbian crowd, the liberal commu-
nists, the supporters of regional causes, the neo-machos,
the naturalist-hippies, the bar poet, the genius, the signer
of petitions who feels validated because he has a 'cause,'
any cause at all, and the dratted sender of e-mails against
whom no anti-virus is good enough, and they all loathe
one another with an intensity unparalleled in any other
sample of the human species, because their so-called gift
with words escalates everything to a state of paranoia,
creating a frightening view of reality. At the same time,
to make everything worse, they're irrelevant individuals
who produce unmarketable flops. Virtually nothing they
write is of any importance and fewer and fewer people
are interested in them—generally only other would-be
writers, intrinsically tiresome individuals, making this
tiny arena of letters an infernal cesspool of nightmares,
frustrations, and revenge. This is the common core—in
appearance they're very different, of course, very decep-
tive. They're even invited to events like this, and the likes
of Linnaeus would have a hard time classifying them
exhaustively, so rich is the fauna. They have an incredible
ability to disguise themselves. A father would walk his
daughter down the aisle to a writer, tickled pink, oblivious to what awaits her. There are the thoughtful writers,
the grotesque ones, the enormously promising, the rude
ones, the unionists, the contest winners, the presidents

of associations, the pornographers, the contest losers, the downright bad ones, the autistic ones, the imitators, the ones who send letters to the editor, the non-writers (who are different from the bad writers) and so on. It's quite obvious: if writers were good people they'd hold a decent job, something truly useful to the brotherhood of man; they'd be normal individuals, capable of getting along and possessing all the humanist values they sing of from time to time, index finger raised, unable to apply them to their own lives. Writing is always an expression of failure, from which nothing is learned—contrary to real life, in which mistakes make us better people. In literature the opposite is true: the sick presumptuousness that leads us to write and that every so often finds some small resonance—the dish of leftover food for the famished dog, which we lunge at with our tongues out—ends up entirely corrupting our souls, so that after a few years we are good for nothing save measuring our own incompetence, line by line."

I paused for effect and took a sip of water from the awful plastic cup with a certain Episcopal poise, to feel the temperature of the Curitiba audience, with which, tragically, I was unfamiliar; it seems the city has an inexplicable reputation for being highbrow. Beside me, the other guest speaker (whose name escapes me), a friendly municipal novelist and university professor who was trying not to laugh, perhaps because he was a victim of that semiformal kind of respect for others that is the mark of the provinces, perhaps because he thought (he doesn't know me) I'd meant what I said and that laughter might offend me. And then, suddenly, I *felt* the audience's icy silence—in a split second I realized that my cynical, absurd diatribe, albeit inspired (I was speaking with the lightness of one who writes, each comma in its place, the rhythm weighed, the gestures discreet but efficient), was being received, or read, as a succession of stones thrown at their heads, and they were trying to work out which frequency to tune my mike to—irony, aggression, humor, stupidity—and I could see in the intrigued eyes of the first row a desperate scrabbling to find the precise way to finally understand what I was saying. They were weighing my every word—in the mortal silence that followed my sip of water—as one might heft a ball of lead in one's hand. No one smiled. I took another sip, slowly, to gain time—I'd clearly got the tone wrong. The other two times I gave practically the same opening speech—at a biennial in Bahia and the Porto Alegre Book Fair—it was received with guffawing, laughter, a shuffling of chairs, people glancing at one another and whispering something, *that's so funny,* or *this guy's really good,* here and there an actively serious face, already rehearsing an argument, and further back a timid protest with a fist in the air, in short, an instant success that quickly occasioned (what one might call "instigating") questions, some frankly provocative, about literature, cynicism, politics, and ethics that put everyone at ease and I practically didn't have to think until the end of the event, just replying with automatic, tried-and-tested answers, to then collect my check and get on with life.

But the silence fell with a thud—pardon the image— on the table. I'd been warned that Curitiba wasn't easy, that I was going to find a stiff-necked lot, hard nuts to crack. But that wasn't it. The audience was great: they'd absorbed exactly what I'd said, and especially *how* I'd said it. Truth was, I'd gotten the tone wrong because I had, in fact, believed each word I'd uttered. I'd committed the mortal sin of not stepping back from myself, and if there is one undisguisable thing in this world it is bitterness, that corrosive, destructive feeling, that malaise without direction or definite object which, on that day, at that moment, had washed right over me. The novelist next to me had felt like laughing because, being an autistic kind of writer, he hadn't listened to me, he'd only read me, and in the abstraction of reading, everything is a game of double meanings and we all skip happily through a garden of forking paths. But not the audience—they'd listened to me and absorbed me completely, clutched at my soul—they were held in thrall by that spectacle of life, by the abyss of the present moment, something of which no writer is capable. Hence the silence. Hence the three people at the back, indistinct shapes in the darkness, getting up and leaving, discreet enough so that the contempt they felt for me wasn't transformed into a "message." But before you think I was illuminated by some superior, insurmountable philosophical sentiment, a Heideggerian crisis, an existential cul-de-sac, a transcendental awareness of the shortcomings of my profession, I should explain why I was so inexplicably swept up in my own words, and the reason was rather like the ultimate proof of my own thesis, that is, the fact that writers really are awful sorts. Afterward—I'd have to rid myself of the novelist first—I was going to have dinner with an old hometown rival, a childhood friend, and also, unfortunately, a writer.

He'd started writing later, when I'd already established a solid reputation for myself, and, unassumingly, he'd published one thing after another, occupying spaces, winning prizes, making friends, writing regular columns, and now miraculously sold ten times more than I did. He appeared everywhere and was invited to everything, while I, who'd practically taken him by the hand to a big publishing house and wrote fifty times better than he did—but I'm going to change the subject; remembering bothers me, I get short of breath, I feel a compulsion to drink. I took a third sip of water, trying to create some new fact in that terrible silence—at precisely that moment I remembered him, our dinner, the superior (superior no; paternalistic, *protective*) tone of voice in which he'd spoken to me— Let's get together! Yes, let's! Man, I've split up with my wife. I've started a new life! I'm so glad you could come to Literary Week! I gave your name a good plug down at the Foundation! They're a bunch of idiots. They don't know anything about literature, you know how it is, the same old story! They didn't even know who you were. I had to tell them. Look, I'm going to choose a good restaurant and I'll meet you at the hotel. What do you say?—I felt the audience darken before me and realized I was bogged down in the silence and crushed by memory; I had to go on, say something, crack a joke, back down, with a cowardly *of course that's just a metaphor but*, but I was unable to: I saw my friend's face in front of me, separated from his wretched wife, a woman who was practically my only trump card; his being married to her—and I was his best man—she was my joy, a really ugly, unpleasant woman, thick as a plank, capable of coming out with the most

absurd statements and making the biggest confessions in
the crowded intimacy of an elevator in a shrill voice hint-
ing at the hysteria of those who are unhappy in the sack—
his being married to her was a form of compensation for
me: OK, let him do what he wants—he already pays
enough for his crimes by sleeping with her every night.
And now he brings me to Curitiba and the first thing he
tells me is that he's split up with his wife and is starting
a new life, at 40, and each of his sentences was overflow-
ing with happiness, a feeling inaccessible to those who
write; I knew what he was going through, it really was
good; after four marriages I knew what the moment after
liberation was like, it was as if the world was beginning
again after those drawn out traumatic experiences that
we subject ourselves to for long periods of time obeying
some kind of uncontrollable atavism, because he was in
that exact moment, and may even have brought me here
(and I accepted that ridiculous fee) just to tell me, to gloat,
always with the excuse that he had my best interests at
heart *because you need it*, the son-of-a-bitch was capable of
telling me. I took one last sip of water and felt a pang of
acidity deep inside—I was taking too long to continue my
speech, the spotlights in the auditorium hurt my eyes, I
could barely see anyone beyond the already uneasy figures
in the front row and the municipal novelist next to me also
began to fidget, I realized—I could almost hear the gears
of his brain working—that he was desperately wondering
how to undo the knot I'd created with my weird silence,
because my face couldn't have looked so great either. It
seemed that until I'd resolved my problem with Cássio—
my childhood friend's name—until I'd rid myself of him

for real, killing him perhaps (and in three seconds I'd come up with an entire narrative about a writer who kills another and is unmasked by his inability to control his own happiness), I wouldn't be able to take a step forward, say a word, any one at all, that might open the gates and enable me to proceed with that tragedy—I was choking. In the darkness (I missed Cássio's wife, importuning him physically and mentally with her mere presence beside him in a bar, but now she wouldn't be there any more to play her role), the novelist, with a professional smile— he had experience in round tables, I noticed—took his microphone, which, of course, didn't work, then asked to borrow mine, gave it two little taps that exploded in the loudspeakers, made a supposedly funny gesture and finally put an end to that paralysis.

"Well, after an unusual introduction by Antonio Donetti, a wonderfully provocative topic for this evening, perhaps it's time to throw open the discussion to questions from the audience and . . . "

I could no longer see a thing, not even Cássio's happy smile; Cássio, single at 40, who would no doubt welcome me with open arms in some trendy restaurant and give me a bear hug—I leaned towards the novelist and whispered in the worst voice I could muster: *I'm not feeling well. Maybe* . . . and there was a commotion of niceties, while part of the audience left grumbling, ten minutes to listen to that shit and then go home, and part sat there stunned, watching the whispering at the table, which was soon surrounded by busybodies; someone even asked if there was a doctor present, but fortunately there wasn't one to diagnose my fraud, and thus, feigning dizziness while

gesticulating *don't worry, it's nothing*, I escaped through
a back door that abruptly left me in a square, Largo da
Ordem, the novelist behind me, genuinely worried—*We
were thinking about going for dinner. Do you think . . .*—but
I wormed my way free, *I'm going to look for a cab, a walk
will do me good, I think it's my stomach, I*, and I told a few
more lies, finally leaving him behind, almost sprinting
away, dashing off in search of fresh air, until I was lying
in the darkness of my hotel room, waiting for the phone
to ring; now I desperately wanted to see him to measure
in loco the pressure that was doing me in and the next
moment—funny, time flew in that state of despair, and
not the opposite, as narrative cliché would have it—the
phone rang violently. *I know what you've been up to*, and
there was a frankly cheerful laugh that spoke for itself
and left me speechless: he was happy. *No*, I said, *you don't
need to pick me up, I'll meet you at the restaurant, that's better*, because it occurred to me that he might promise me
a lift, then leave me waiting in front of the hotel for two
hours, and not turn up, as a kind of payback. So off I
went to meet him, and if he wasn't there I'd sit and eat
a nice dinner and we'd never speak again until the end
of time, which would be liberating. But there he was, of
course. That's why he'd brought me for that ridiculous
talk that I'd forcefully hurled into the air and which was
now beginning to come back down in my soul with all the
force of gravity to crush me till the end of time. To speak
is to reveal oneself; to write is to conceal, I thought when
I saw him slowly stand smiling behind a table swathed in
half-light, next to the silhouette of a woman, and I froze.
Instead of his hideous wife who was no doubt now taking

care of their two small children, living off puny alimony payments because she didn't know how to do anything, I saw the face of a beautiful woman, a young woman, with short, straight, fair hair that was the oval frame of a calm, down-to-earth face, from whose smile emerged happy, white teeth as soon as I drew near, while she got up from the table with the litheness of a nymph—*Please, don't get up*, and I touched her hand with both of mine—*Cássio, it's so good to see you again*, and I vigorously shook his calloused hand to rid myself of the instantaneous memory of her skin, *Alice, this is my friend Alice*, and his smile was one of those high points in life that we will never get back again, I felt that this was the cliché he inhabited now; and the next minute the waiter was offering me the menu and asking something that I refused to hear in order to get a better look at Alice's eyes, *She owns an editorial agency, and she also translates from English, French, and Italian*, which got a smile out of her, simulating an inhibition that may actually have been real, the gesture saying something like *oh come on, Cássio, don't exaggerate, I just* and he kept talking—I'll join them in some wine, I told the waiter so he'd leave—about Alice's qualities, and how he intended to introduce her to a new publishing house in São Paulo, *this girl's a gem*, and I immediately agreed, shocked at how stupid Cássio was for spoiling her in such a merciless and vulgar manner like that; but suddenly, soon after our toast I felt that that terrible source of unhappiness—seeing him so happy beside a gorgeous woman—was also its antidote, my elixir of youth, *stealing her from him*, which gave me a whole mission in life concocted in the few seconds following the toast in which I noticed the intensity of Alice's gaze, which I still hadn't translated, until I saw her, deliciously flustered, open her bag—while Cássio went white, stuttering a sudden change of subject *But what exactly did you say at the talk, they called me, you*—and hand me an old copy of my first book, *The Photo in the Mirror*, deaf to any other subject.

"I was telling Cássio, I didn't know he knew you personally. I love this book. I've read it three times. Could you autograph it for me?" she asked. And shyly recognizing her inopportune gesture, "It's just that I don't want to forget."

"Of course, Alice!" And it was Cássio himself, seething with jealousy—which seemed absurd and thus even more ridiculous—who handed me a pen, because I lied and said I didn't have one on me just so he'd have to complete the mechanical gesture of offering me one, which I happily accepted, while writing a short dedication with his crappy ballpoint, beneath and inspired by Alice's gaze. Cássio was yesterday's news—he'd faded into the background, never to emerge again, I figured—I'd wrench Alice from his arms, and without much effort, a fine revenge, the redeeming kind; what a wonderful trip to Curitiba, I'd stay another month, a year, whatever it took, and it was Alice herself who was giving me all the cues, mesmerized by the memory of a book she'd read three times and which was now taking shape as if by miracle in my easygoing, friendly, smiling persona, before her very eyes, like a gift. *So you're in the editorial business—that's funny, I've been looking for a proofreader with a feel for literature, which is very rare, more than a proofreader, an interlocutor*—and she stared at me with such intensity at the mere idea—

someone I could use as a sounding board, more than just, you know? Sometimes, I look at a paragraph and I—I could hear heavy breathing; it was Cássio, civilized, still struggling to keep up appearances, strong enough to play along with my cruelty for the sake of politeness—*Yes, Alice is brilliant, she*—but no one was interested in what he had to say anymore. *Of course, let's talk, I'd love to, I*—and Alice handed me her card, which was charmingly simple, *Alice, Editorial Assistance.*

"Shall we start tomorrow?"

"Yes, let's!"

I finally opened the menu: fillet steak with garlic and oil, no, not today; fillet steak cooked in butter, medium rare, with a side salad. *And there you are*, I thought, before the new toast. Alice's green eyes were glistening.

Translated by Alison Entrekin

Translators

ALEXIS LEVITIN has translated 26 books, including Astrid Cabral's *Cage*, Clarice Lispector's *Soulstorm*, and Eugénio de Andrade's *Forbidden Words*. He is a recipient of two NEA translation fellowships and two Fulbright Lectureships. In addition, Levitin has been a resident at the Banff International Literary Translation Centre, the European Translators Collegium in Germany, and the Rockefeller Foundation retreat in Bellagio, Italy. His translations have appeared in over 200 magazines, including *Kenyon Review, New England Review, Partisan Review, Prairie Schooner,* and *American Poetry Review*. His most recent book is a cotranslation of *Tapestry of the Sun: An Anthology of Contemporary Ecuadorian Poetry*.

GREGORY RABASSA has translated several major Latin American novelists from both Spanish and Portuguese, including Julio Cortázar, Jorge Amado, and Gabriel García Márquez. On the advice of Cortázar, García Márquez waited three years for Rabassa's schedule to become open so that he could translate *One Hundred Years of Solitude*. He later declared Rabassa's translation to be superior to his own Spanish original. Typically, Rabassa translates without reading the book beforehand, working as he goes. For his version of Cortázar's novel, *Hopscotch*, Rabassa received a National Book Award for Translation. Rabassa currently teaches at Queens College, where he is a Distinguished Professor. In 2006, he was awarded the National

Medal of Arts. His book detailing his experiences as a translator, *If This Be Treason: Translation and Its Dyscontents, A Memoir,* was published by New Directions in 2006.

~

CRISTINA FERREIRA-PINTO BAILEY was born in Rio de Janeiro and teaches in the Department of Romance Languages at Washington & Lee University. Her books include *Gender, Discourse and Desire in Twentieth-Century Brazilian Women's Literature* (2004) and *Poemas da vida meia* (2002). She translated Ignácio de Loyola Brandão's novel *Teeth Under the Sun* (Dalkey, 2007) and poetry and stories by Marina Colasanti and Sonia Coutinho, some of which have have appeared in *Subtropics* and in *Witness*. She is also the editor of the anthology *Urban Voices: Contemporary Short Stories from Brazil* (1999).

PAMELA G. BIRD has translated from Portuguese two books by Brazilian writer José J. Veiga, *The Three Trials of Manirema* and *The Misplaced Machine and Other Stories*, from which the present selection was drawn.

ALBERT BORK has translated and published a great variety of work from Portuguese and Spanish: Brazilian novels, film scripts, essays, and poems; Mexican and Spanish history; Cuban short stories; and Latin American art criticism. He headed the translation department of a Texas state agency for 17 years and has been the official court interpreter at the Alpine, Texas, U.S. Federal Court since June 2001.

MARGARET JULL COSTA has been a literary translator for over 20 years and has translated many novels and short stories by Portuguese, Spanish, and Latin American writers, including Javier Marías, Fernando Pessoa, and José Saramago. In 2008 she won the PEN Book-of-the-Month Translation Award and the Oxford Weidenfeld Translation Prize for her version of Eça de Queiroz's masterpiece *The Maias.*

ALISON ENTREKIN has translated a number of works by Brazilian and Portuguese authors into English, including *City of God*, by Paulo Lins, *The Day I Killed My Father*, by Mario Sabino, and *Budapest*, by Chico Buarque, which was shortlisted for the 2004 Independent Foreign Fiction Prize in the UK. Originally from Australia, she now lives in Brazil.

DAVID GEORGE is a professor of modern languages and literature at Lake Forest College in Illinois. He is an expert on Brazilian theater and Latin American literature, which he teaches and writes about. He has published many articles in English, Spanish, and Portuguese, books in English and Portuguese, and has translated several books, short stories, and plays. He has received grants from the National Endowment for the Humanities, Social Science Research Council, Fulbright Commission, and the American Council of Learned Societies.

CLIFFORD LANDERS, professor emeritus at New Jersey City University, has translated more than 20 book-length works from Portuguese, including novels by Rubem Fonseca, Jorge Amado, João Ubaldo Ribeiro, Patrícia Melo, José de Alencar, Chico Buarque, António Lobo Antunes, Nélida Piñon, Paulo Coelho, and Marcos Rey. A recipient of the Mario Ferreira Award and a National Endowment for the Arts grant for prose translation, he is author of *Literary Translation: A Practical Guide*.

NAOMI LINDSTROM is a professor of Spanish, Portuguese, Latin American Studies, and Comparative Literature and a member of the Schusterman Center for Jewish Studies at the University of Texas at Austin. Her books include *Early Spanish American Narrative, The Social Conscience of Latin American Writing,* and *Jewish Issues in Argentine Literature*. She manages the Web site and Listserv of the Latin American Jewish Studies Association (LAJSA).

JOHNNY LORENZ, the son of Brazilian immigrants, is an English professor at Montclair State University. He has published poetry and translations in numerous journals and was awarded a Fulbright to translate and study the work of Mario Quintana, whose poetry he discovered through his grandmother. Quintana is not as well known abroad as he is in Brazil, but Lorenz hopes to change that.

ELIZABETH LOWE is director of the Center for Translation Studies at the University of Illinois at Urbana-Champaign. She is also the co-author of a book on translation and the rise in inter-American literature. Among her many translations is Joaquim Machado de Assis's

Esau and Jacob for Oxford University Press. Her current project is a retranslation of Euclides da Cunha's *Os Sertões*.

MALCOLM MCNEE teaches at Smith College. He is co-editor of *Gilberto Freyre e os estudos latinoamericanos,* and his essays on Lusophone literatures and cultures appear in journals in Brazil, Portugal, the United States, and Britain. His current research focuses on representations of rural place and subjectivity in contemporary Brazilian literature and visual culture. These are his first published literary translations.

BARBARA SHELBY MERELLO is a retired Foreign Service officer who has lived in Peru, Spain, Mexico, Brazil, Argentina, Ecuador, and Costa Rica. She has translated several of Jorge Amado's works, including *Tent of Miracles, Tieta,* and *Tereza Batista: Home from the Wars.*

LUIZA FRANCO MOREIRA is an associate professor of Comparative Literature at Binghamton University. Her specialization is Brazilian Modernism and its relation to the Estado Novo dictatorship. An active translator and poet, she edited a collection of Cassiano Ricardo's poetry. She is the author of *Meninos, Poetas e Héróis* (*Children, Poets, and Heroes*), which is a study of Ricardo's written works, and has contributed scholarly articles to various journals and anthologies.

LYNNE REAY PEREIRA has been involved in several translation projects from Portuguese to English, including the National Library Foundation Translation Support Programme and the Bei /Unibanco guides to Brazil and individual regions. She is also a regular translator for the Portogente Web site. Originally from England, she now lives in Brazil, where she runs an English school with her Brazilian husband.

PEGGY L. SHARPE is a professor of Portuguese at Florida State University where she also teaches courses on Brazilian literature, cinema, and culture. The recipient of two Fulbright awards to Brazil, she has written, edited, and translated numerous books and scholarly articles, including several on the subject of Brazilian women writers of the 19th and 20th centuries.

K.C.S. SOTELINO has a BA from Stanford University and an MA and PhD in Literature from the University of California in Santa Cruz. Her translations have appeared in numerous Brazilian magazines and books, as well as in *Beacons*. She has also published articles about translation in *Revista de Letras*, *Tempo e Memória*, and *Hispania*. She is currently a visiting scholar in the Division of Humanities at Stanford University.

ELLEN DORÉ WATSON is at work on a second book of Adélia Prado's poetry, having already translated *The Alphabet in the Park*. Director of the Poetry Center at Smith College, Watson has published four collections of poems including *This Sharpening*, and was dubbed by *Library Journal* as one of the "24 Poets for the 21st Century." Recipient of an NEA Translation Fellowship, Watson is the poetry and translation editor of *The Massachusetts Review*.

RICHARD ZENITH's translations range from medieval poetry to contemporary writing and include several titles by Portuguese writer Fernando Pessoa, such as *The Book of Disquiet*. His *Education by Stone: Selected Poems of João Cabral de Melo Neto* won the Landon Translation Award from the Academy of American Poets. Among his translations are four novels by Antonio Lobo Antunes and the recently released *Sonnets and Other Poems* by Luis de Camões.

Acknowledgments

First of all, I would like to thank Leonor Scliar-Cabral and Astrid Cabral, two poet friends from Brazil, who gave me kind hospitality and extensive advice on authors to be included in this collection. In addition, I would like to thank all the translators who agreed to contribute to this anthology. In particular, I wish to thank Alison Entrekin in Santos, Brazil, for untiring efforts in providing a variety of short stories from various regions to help round off this collection. Most important of all, I wish to express my gratitude to my colleague and old friend, Clifford Landers, who, in addition to providing numerous translations for this book, welcomed me into his home with its rich Brazilian library in Naples, Florida, where, during two weeks of sunshine and hard work, we gave this book its final form. As for Gregory Rabassa, *il miglior fabbro,* I am deeply grateful not just for his willingness to contribute a foreword to this book, but for the cheerful and generous support he has given me throughout my translating career. I would like to thank the State University of New York at Plattsburgh for its ongoing sponsorship of my translation activities. I would like to thank the editors of the following magazines in which stories in this anthology, sometimes under slightly different titles, had their first appearance in English translation:

Cadernos de Literatura em Tradução	"The Cage"
Central Park	"The Flying Man"
Grand Street	"Truth is a Seven-Headed Beast" and "Those Lopes"
Latin American Literary Review	"Plaza Mauá"
The Ohio Journal	"Shaving"
The Review	"Architect by Correspondence"
Webster Review	"The Dead Man in the Sea at Urca"
Harper's Magazine	"The Miracle of the Birds"

Permissions

The following are listed in order of appearance in this book. Every effort has been made to identify the holders of copyright of previously published material included in this book; any errors that may have been made will be corrected in subsequent printings upon notification to the publisher. The following permissions list reflects the order the stories appear in this book.

Luis Fernando Verissimo's "The Real José" (original title "O Verdadeiro José" in *As Mentiras Que Os Homens Contam*) Editora Objetiva, Rio de Janeiro, RJ © 2000 by Luis Fernando Verissomo. English © 2010 by Margaret Jull Costa.

Machado de Assis's "The Wallet" was published by permission of Alison Entrekin. English © 2010 Alison Entrekin.

Rubem Fonseca's "Account of the Incident" is reprinted by courtesy of the author and the translator, Clifford E. Landers.

Adriana Lisboa's "Altitude" is reprinted by permission of the translator, Malcolm McNee.

Clarice Lispector's "The Dead Man in the Sea at Urca" and "Plaza Mauá" are reprinted by permission of New Directions Publishing Corp. Translated by Alexis Levitin, from *Soulstorm*, © 1974 by Clarice Lispector, English © 1989 by Alexis Levitin.

Helena Parente Cunha's "The Traffic Light" was reprinted by permission of the translator, Naomi E. Lindstrom, and the University Press of America, and originally appeared in *Urban Voices*, edited by Christina Ferreira-Pinto.

Sonia Coutinho's "Josete Killed Herself" is published courtesy of the translator, Cristina Ferreira-Pinto Bailey.

Paula Parisot's "Ipanema Is a Long Way from Home" was translated and published by permission of the author and the translator. English © 2010 Elizabeth Lowe. Original © Paula Parisot.

Fred Góes's "A Thing of Beauty" is reprinted by permission of the translator, Clifford E. Landers.

Julieta de Godoy Ladeira's "The Virtuous Wife" is reprinted by permission of the translator, David S. George.

Marcos Rey's "Architect by Correspondence" is reprinted by permission of the translator, Cliff Landers.

Álvaro Cardoso Gomes's "The Piece" was translated and published by permission of the author and the translator, Karen C. S. Sotelino. English © 2010 Karen S. C. Sotelino.

Fernando Bonassi's "Chilly Night" (translated by Luiza Franco Moreira) was reprinted by permission of the translator and the University Press of America, and originally appeared in *Urban Voices,* edited by Christina Ferreira-Pinto.

Luiz Ruffato's "Taxi" was published by permission of the author and Alison Entrekin. English © 2010 Alison Entrekin.

Benedicto Monteiro's "The Saint and the City" and "Sunset" are translated and published by permission of the translator, Albert G. Bork. English © 2010 Albert G. Bork.

Astrid Cabral's "Claws Revealed" was translated and published by permission of the author and the translator, Alexis Levitin. English © 2010 Alexis Levitin.

Milton Hatoum's "Truth Is a Seven-Headed Beast" is reprinted by permission of the translator, Ellen Doré Watson.

Marcia Denser's "The Last Tango in Jacobina" was reprinted by permission of the University Press of America, and originally appeared in *Urban Voices,* edited by Christina Ferreira-Pinto, and by Peggy Sharpe.

Jorge Amado's "The Miracle of the Birds" is reprinted by permission of Harper's Magazine. English © 1982 by Harper's Magazine. All Rights reserved. Reproduced from the April issue by special permission.

João Ubaldo Ribeiro's "Carnival Traumas" is reprinted by permission of the translator, Clifford E. Landers.

Flávio Carneiro's "The Pageant" was published by permission of Alison Entrekin. English © 2010 Alison Entrekin.

Adélia Prado's "Rituals" and "Santinha and Me" were reprinted by permission of the translator Ellen Watson.

Augusta Faro's "The Cage" was published by permission of the author and Alison Entrekin. English © 2010 Alison Entrekin.

Adriana Lisboa's "Rediscovery" and "Geography" are reprinted by permission of the translator, Malcolm McNee.

Luiz Vilela's "Shaving" was translated and published by permission of the author. English © 2010 Alexis Levitin.

J. J. Veiga's "The Misplaced Machine" was reprinted by permission of the author and the translator, Albert G. Bork.

Guimarães Rosa's "Those Lopes" reprinted by permission of the translator and Oxford University Press.

Simões Lopes Neto's "The Old Ox" is published by permission of the translator, Johnny Lorenz. © 2010 Johnny Lorenz. Originally published in Portuguese in 1912.

Moacyr Scliar's "A Barbecue Story" is reprinted by permission of the translator, Clifford E. Landers.

Pena Cabreira's "Loss" is reprinted by permission of the translator, Clifford E. Landers.

Rodrigo de Haro's "The Flying Man" is translated and published by permission of the author and the translator, Alexis Levitin. English © 2010 Alexis Levitin.

Dalton Trevisan's "The Elephants' Graveyard" was reprinted courtesy of Gregory Rabassa. Originally published in Portuguese as *Cemitério de Elefantes*, by Editôra Civilização Brasileira, S.A., Rio de Janeiro. English © 1972 by Alfred A. Knopf, Inc.

Cristovão Tezza's "Alice and the Writer": was published by permission of the author and Alison Entrekin. English © 2010 Alison Entrekin.